Bass Buff

A Striper Fishing Obsession Guide

by

Captain Tom Mikoleski

Graphic Design by Elena L. Mikoleski
Edited by William A. Muller

Printed in the United States of America

I dedicate this book to the love of my life, my best friend, and my wife, Elena Hidalgo Mikoleski. This book has been on the fringes of my mind for many years. In 2011, Elena pushed me "to put up or shut up." Elena simply lives with my striper obsession, and has never tried to change me. What more could I ask for?

Acknowledgements

I would like to acknowledge the following people who have helped me get to a very happy place in my life.

First, I would like to thank my mom and dad, Regina and Benjamin Mikoleski. I wish they could have witnessed the day I was promoted to Sergeant while on the NYPD. I'm sure they would have been very proud, and I also believe they would have been equally proud to see this book in print. Both my parents have been gone a long time. However, rarely does a day go by without me thinking of them. I miss them very much, and dearly wish I could have one more day on the water fishing with my dad.

Next would have to be my brother, Captain Peter Mikoleski of the *Miss Mac*. Pete and I have spent many great, and some not so great fishing trips together. Sadly, today we hardly ever get to fish together because we are always running our individual boat's. Pete took the plunge and spent his hard earned cash on a rickety old runabout many years ago. If this had never happened, who knows how involved in fishing I'd be today. I would also like to thank Pete for pushing me to get my captain's license, and also for all the times he let me "borrow" the *Regina M* and *Miss Mac*.

Keeping with the family I would like to thank all my uncles and cousins who I've fished with over the years. I can clearly recall many cherished fishing trips, especially those with my uncles: Frank Maciewski, and Ed (Chink) Mikoleski. Cousins: Robert, Richard, and Michael Wesolowski, and Frankie, and Laura Jendresky Gallego.

A very special thank you goes to my long time friend Bill "Doc" Muller. Bill is responsible for me becoming both a better angler and writer. He diligently encouraged me through the entire writing process of this book. Along the way, he was extremely patient with me as I struggled to polish my words into clear, concise sentences. I'm eternally grateful for all the time and effort Bill put into this project to bring it up to his high standards. I have no doubt this book would never have been completed without Bill's assistance.

Next, is my dear friend and legendary angler, Captain Bob Rocchetta of the *Rainbow*. Captain Bob set me on the proper course of striper fishing as a young teenager, and without knowing it, he also guided me to become a better man. Shortly after I graduated from the NYPD Academy, we met up at some local outdoor show, and Bob told me how proud he was of me. I never forgot those words. I know I'll never be in Bob's league when it comes to being a fisherman. However, someday I hope to catch a striper larger than his current NYS record of 76-pounds. In reality, I have a better shot at winning the Lottery, but I know if I ever pull it off, Bob will be the first one to congratulate me.

I would also like to acknowledge Fred Golofaro, Editorial Director of *The Fisherman Magazine*. Not only has Fred taught me a lot about fishing, he also had the kindness to print an article from a teenage kid (me) way back in the 80's. I have no doubt that this simple act laid the groundwork for this entire book.

Much appreciation would also have to go to Author Angelo Peluso, and Doctor Jim House. Their kind words were significant, and encouraged me to forge ahead and complete this project.

Thanks must go to my dear friends and mates who make my job much easier aboard the *Grand Slam*: Captain Wayne Hermann, Captain Erik Weingartner, Captain Steve Kull, Captain Derek Grattan, and Kenny Leon.

I would also like to acknowledge in alphabetical order the following Captains for their assistance to me while "out on the water": Mike Boccio *Prime Time lll*, Frank Busuttil *Sonny Boy*, Rick Etzel *Breakaway*, Carl Forsberg *Viking Fleet*, Jimmy George *Nicole Marie*,

Al Giglio *Gingeral*, Kenny Hejducek *My Joyce*, Richie Jensen *Nancy Ann IV*, Phil Kess *Fishy Business*, Jim Krug *Persuader*, Ron Lajda *Coyote*, Bo Malinowski *Night Stalker*, Joe McBride *My Mate*, Jim Montalbano *Montyman II*, Jeff Nichols *Second Choice*, Larry Perlaki *Sonny Boy*, Steve Phillips *Donna*, Steve Rowland *Professional Crier*, Skip Rudolph *Adios*, Scott Shapiro *Scott Free*, Rick Vidal *Devocean*, Mike Vegessi *Lazy Bones*, and Chris Vitucci *Sea Dancer*.

I would also like to acknowledge the entire staff at Gone Fishing Marina, especially Tom and Maureen Sennefelder. Gone Fishing is my home away from home whenever I'm in Montauk, and from day one, I have been treated with great respect by the whole crew.

Finally, I would like to thank my loyal charter clients who continue to encourage my Striper Fishing Obsession.

CONTENTS

FORWARD

I've been fortunate enough to have lived my whole life around the water. I've worked on it, discovered under it, and pretty much enjoyed being on it, as many ways as humanly possible. Somewhere along the line, probably because of nuggets of knowledge handed down to me from family and friends, and also from the writings of great saltwater anglers, I've been told I'm one of Long Island's foremost fishermen. I love being successful as a fishermen. I also love experiencing the joy when others are successful as fishermen while fishing with me. It's true, a beautiful sunrise or sunset, and a wonderful day on the water, all have their unique merits. But, for most fishermen it's the bend of the rod, the excitement of the fight, and everything else involved with getting it right that makes fishing a special time in one's life.

It was from the pens of men like Ernest Hemingway, Nick Karas, and Al Ristori who wrote books and columns for famed magazines like *The Saltwater Sportsman* or the *Long Island Fisherman* that early on helped guide me on the proper path to becoming a successful fisherman. Trust me, without the knowledge of when, where, and how to fish, you better like looking at sunrises and sunsets because that's about all you'll be doing. For being successful, and putting a few in the box to enjoy with family and friends as food on the table, one must be seriously dedicated and knowledgeable of this quest.

Tommy Mikoleski was a young man when I first met him. I knew right away from his curiosity, and ability to listen that he was on the right track to becoming a successful fisherman. As the years passed by, I witnessed his progression as both captain and writer. Through his writings I always admired his ability to explain many of the correct principles about fishing. As time continues to move on, I truly believe Tommy will become one of the more recognized writers within the world of saltwater fishing. Tommy's first book will not only help you learn and laugh, but it will also help you appreciate the man as he shares an important part of his life with us.

I know it's not easy to be a good fisherman, and I'm sure it's even harder to be a good writer. However, Capt. Tom has proven to me time and again his ability to do both successfully, and this book is no different.

Good luck and tight lines to all.

Capt. Bob Rocchetta, *Rainbow Charters*
IGFA World Record Setter, Accomplished Tournament Winner

There have been lots of books written about Striped Bass Fishing. Most of them are full of information on rods, reels, hooks, baits etc. These books might lead you down the path to glory, but none will tell you what it really takes, and how it truly feels to make that journey!

Captain Tom's book is full of everything you need to know in order to catch striped bass consistently: the history, the tools, the techniques, the strategies, and then…there's more. It's also about one of "New York's Finest," who successfully transitioned from patrolling the tough neighborhoods of New York City, to his dream job, patrolling the East End waters of Long Island as one of Montauk's Finest!

Sit down, read this book, and when you do, grab a pen and paper in order to take some notes because you won't be able to absorb it all the first time around. Then, each season, just before the full moon in June, I suggest you read it again. This way all the tips revealed will be fresh in your mind, and you can't help but be a better striper fisherman because of them. However, as Captain Tom advises, please release a good portion of the big cows you land. This way, many striper anglers will have a chance at experiencing the joyfulness that comes from tangling with the mighty, majestic striper.

Captain Peter Mikoleski, *Miss Mac Charters*

"The charm of fishing is that it is the pursuit of what is elusive but attainable, a perpetual series of occasions for hope." -
John Buchan

"If people concentrated on the really important things in life, there'd be a shortage of fishing poles." -
Doug Larson

"Thank you, dear God, for this good life and forgive us if we do not love it enough. Thank you for the rain. And for the chance to wake up in three hours and go fishing: I thank you for that now, because I won't feel so thankful then." -
Garrison Keillor

INTRODUCTION

A person is very lucky if they love their job. I'm pleased to say, I'm now a very lucky person because I run the Montauk charter boat *Grand Slam*. This was not always the case because for 20-years previous I was a member of two New York City Law Enforcement Departments. This initial career choice may have delayed my "luck" for a period of time, but being "on the job" gave me the opportunity to retire at a relatively young age. So, in 2006 I switched professions to pursue my long simmering obsession with the striped bass. An obsession with a fish may seem strange to normal people. However, in my world, it was destiny a long time coming.

Over the years, as my striper fishing obsession developed, I started writing fishing articles. To date, more than one hundred of my articles have been printed in various outdoor magazines. Eventually, the idea of writing a book about my striper obsession began to brew in my mind. However, I was never quite sure I had a whole book in me, so I procrastinated on this project for several years. Fortunately, during that time, I met many anglers who enjoyed reading my articles. These anglers were always complimentary, and conservations would often end with, "So, Captain Tom, when are you going to write a book?" Well, thanks very much for the encouragement, and...**here it is!**

In Part I, I'm going to make it clear why striper fishing is such an obsession for me. Be careful reading these pages because you might see a little bit of me... in you. This section will also include the up to date biology and history of the striped bass. Often, anglers who fish with me have many questions pertaining to the striped bass, and many of the more commonly asked questions will be answered within this section also. In Part II, I will outline precise instructions on how to become a better striped bass fisherman, and in the process, many of my fishing secrets will be revealed to all.

Striped bass fishing has an overpowering hold on me, and during the prime months of the season I simply live and breathe everything striped bass. In fact, my biggest anxiety when large stripers are swimming in my home waters is the fear of not being on the water during the hottest bite of the season. I know I'm not alone in such thoughts. And with heartfelt respect, this book is written for all other anglers who share similar feelings because I assure you, I feel your pain. So read on, and *take a ride* into my striper fishing obsession.

You might have a striper obsession if…

- You continue to fish even when your body aches from long hours at the rail

- Your hands and fingers are scraped raw from unhooking too many stripers

- Aspirin comes along on every trip just to dull the aches and pains caused from the above

- Vacation time is scheduled in order to take advantage of moon tides

- During the fall run sleep and food are optional

- Time of day is irrelevant when the tide is right

- Pondering new striper tactics causes insomnia

- Losing a big striper mentally hurts

- You'll drive miles for fresh bait, and once there, you hand pick individual pieces

- You have saved a hook or lure because it caught a particularly large striper for you

- You hide your hot lures and rigs before getting to the dock, so no one sees them

- You leave the dock, and the sun is in the west… you return to the dock, and the sun is in the east

- You start checking the marine forecast on Monday for Saturday's trip

- You commonly check the marina fish cleaning dumpster to see the "rack size" of stripers being caught

- You view a full moon, and striper fishing immediately pops into your head

- You realize the more you know about striper fishing, the more you don't know

PART I

Chapter 1

Long Way from Queens to Montauk

How does a kid who grew up in Queens, New York become a Montauk charter boat captain? I was born in 1964, and I believe within hours of my birth my father Ben, and older brother Pete must have taken me fishing. As I grew older I discovered that I had many uncles and cousins who were also fishermen.

So, whenever we got together for family events the topic of fishing was sure to come up. Fluke and flounder were my father's favorite fish to catch, so flat fish were usually our main fishing targets, but sometimes we also caught blue claw crabs and snapper blues.

Top:
Me and my cousin, Laura, with one of her first stripers

Left:
My father, Benny Mikoleski, with a double header of flounder caught in Reynold's Channel

I was too young to experience the heyday of striped bass fishing during the 70's. In fact, in my early fishing years I never caught a striped bass and neither did my father, or brother. I never even saw a real live striper until the early 80's. Regardless, we were often successful anglers, and depending on the stage of the season our 5-gallon bucket was normally filled with something good to eat.

Rarely, if ever, was a fish released during my younger years that were big enough to keep. A big reason for this hoarding was probably the "Depression Era Mentality" that thrived not only in my father's way of thinking, but also in many other fishermen that came from his generation. Mind you, none of our catch ever went to waste, but catch and release fishing was simply not on the agenda.

My father loved eating whole fried flounder and fluke. He would simply scale the bodies, cut the head off, remove the innards, and have my mom, Regina, bread the fish and fry them. My mother fried with Crisco, a white lard that looked like wall spackle to me. Back then there were no gourmet oils to enhance the flavor of the catch. Personally, this cooking method turned me off, but almost every Friday the aroma of fried fish could be smelled wafting from our house.

In the 70's my dad used to take my brother and me fishing frequently. At that time there were no size or bag limits on winter flounder, and fluke had to be 14-inches to keep, but they also had no bag limit. Neither species had seasons, so when they were biting we simply went fishing for them. My father has long passed. However, if he was around today to witness the winter flounder collapse, and the strict regulations on an abundant species like fluke, it would have frustrated him greatly. In fact, I doubt my father would have bothered to go fishing in today's world. As a result, I often wonder today how different my life would be if this had been the case.

During my early teens it was touch and go, mainly because I was hanging out with the wrong crowd. My mother could see problems developing, and had many talks with me, but her advice often fell on deaf ears. My father continued to guide me in his own quiet way, but still I gradually turned away from productive activities such as sports and fishing.

Perhaps, the defining moment for me came the night I was jumped by a group of thugs from an adjoining neighborhood that were looking to settle a score with some of my friends. Evidently, the main targets for the retaliation were nowhere to be found, and the fact that I had nothing to do with their "beef" was irrelevant to these marauding a-holes. So when they found me hanging out on the corner of my house, I simply became the convenient target to receive a beating. I got banged up pretty good, and to this day, I can still recall the impacts of a baseball bat and crowbar to the left side of my body. Somehow, I bolted away from the group, and managed to get the hell out of Dodge before my skull was cracked open. It was definitely time to switch my acquaintances.

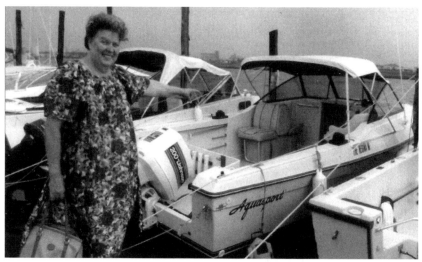

My mom, Regina, points at the Regina M, *named in her honor.*

My father kept me occupied by having me work with him as a helper on his construction jobs. The pay was good, but the work was…work, and I was not too fond of this tough manual labor. Years later I realized I'd blown the chance at learning a great trade because my father was indeed one of the best cement and brick craftsmen around. In fact, even today when I visit relatives in the old neighborhood I often pass by jobs we worked on together 30-years ago, and they still look fantastic.

Working with my dad did help me grow up, but during these times I was never a happy camper. We never had major blowouts with each other, but he was a perfectionist, and I was simply there for the paycheck, so conflicts were sure to occur. However, I dearly treasure the time we spent fishing together. My dad was 44-years old when I was born, a WWII vet, and had a bad back that usually hurt severely. Still, he often found the time and energy to take me fishing. I have no doubt this simple act kept me out of a lot of trouble.

My dad and his buddy, Victor, with a nice catch of flounder in East Rockaway.

In 1981 I got a job at Herman's World of Sporting Goods, and was attending CUNY, Queens College. Around this time I had changed my gaggle of friends, got back into sports, and began playing softball on team called the *Gladiators*. Members of this team were a much better bunch of guys that included my brother and lifelong friend Phil Rizzo. This was also about the time when Pete and I began to smooth out any big brother-little brother conflicts that used to occur because of the ten year difference between us. As I look back, this is also when our mutual obsession for the striped bass began to rise to the next level.

Our quest to catch stripers eventually took us to some diverse fishing spots within the confines of New York. We fished mostly from shore, but sometimes from a boat, and we ended up dropping lines in all the Long Island South Shore bays. In due course, we also tried the North Shore, specifically Little Neck Bay, and also the waters off City and Hart Islands. Road trips to more varied areas, such as Croton on the Hudson and to the Spuyten Duyvil Bridge on the northern tip of Manhattan were also made. I still remember this later trip distinctly. It was a cold dank March day, and the neighborhood we were in was pretty sketchy. Minutes after arriving, I'd wished I had brought two additional "rods" with me, one 9-ft long for extra casting distance, and the other a .45 semi-automatic pistol for protection. In spite of my jitters, it was here, I saw my first live striper when my brother landed a 26-incher on a yellow bucktail.

My dad had no interest in wasting his time and effort to catch striped bass. In fact, I recall a time when Pete and I trailered our 22-ft Aquasport, *Regina M*, out to Montauk in order to fish the "promised land" for a few days. My dad later drove out alone to meet us. The first morning after he arrived I attempted to wake him to get on the boat. He took one look at the clock that read 5:00 A.M., rolled over and mumbled, *"Get up now...to catch a friggin fish? You two are cuckoo!"*

Our early attempts to catch stripers were pitiful, and this lack of success had my father further questioning our sanity. He simply couldn't understand why we wasted so much time catching nothing. Regardless, I'm sure he was happy I was spending more time with my older brother, who always seemed to have his head screwed on pretty straight. However, that morning in Montauk my dad had managed to sum up our obsession quite concisely because we were indeed cuckoo about catching a striper: specifically a big striper.

By the time Pete and I were totally immersed into striper fishing the fishery was about ready to collapse. Yes, there were still large fish being caught, but these fish were not remotely easy to catch. If smaller fish are missing from any fishery it's almost impossible for novices to break down the learning curve. Don't get me wrong, occasionally novices do go out and catch a big fish, but this success has a lot to do with lady luck, and as for us, we were having no luck at all.

In spite of this, our striper fever never waned and we fished for them at every opportunity, but still our catches were meek. Looking back, it is no surprise that we were "bass-less" because we were "clueless" about what it really took to catch the crafty stripers. We knew from reading the *Long Island Fisherman* that bass fishing was good at night, but for some reason we rarely set forth under the cover of darkness. Maybe our parents had a say in that matter, and that was probably a good thing for safety reasons. In hindsight, I guess what we really needed was a mentor.

I still vividly recall the beautifully clear night of July 17, 1981. I was sitting on my front stoop, that's a porch to all you non-city folk, and was watching the slow advancement of a full lunar eclipse. By now I had begun to slightly unravel the striper puzzle. During that night, as a bright full moon gradually dimmed behind the earth's shadow, I remember predicting to myself, *someone is going to catch a big striper tonight.*

Days later, as I diligently read my new copy of the *Long Island Fisherman*, I discovered that Captain Bob Rocchetta had recently crushed the previous world record striper of 73-pounds. Captain Bob's huge bass tugged the scale down to an eye-popping 76-pounds. This was indeed big news in the angling world because the old IGFA record had been in place since 1913. As I read and devoured the information about the catch, I discovered that Captain Bob's striper had indeed been caught on the very night of my prediction, and it was bested in the fabled waters of Montauk, NY. This big fish only poured fuel on the fire of my striper obsession.

Captain Bob Rocchetta with his 76-pound world record striped bass caught in 1981.

My brother tilted the odds in our favor when in the winter of 1982 he booked a charter with Capt. Bob Rocchetta for the coming June. In May, on my 18th birthday, Pete gave this trip to me as a gift. The wait for my first charter fishing trip was torture, but eventually the date arrived.

I remember leaving home in Pete's white 4-door Plymouth Volare' sometime during mid-morning. The drive to the East End without traffic took us a little more than 2-hours. Imagine that, no traffic while driving through the lovely hamlets of Water Mill, Bridge Hampton, or East Hampton. What a concept!

We checked in at the Snug Harbor Hotel and decided to get some lunch. I remember having burgers at West Lake Lodge. The quality of the meal escapes me now, but that could be because of the 600-pound mako shark that was hanging just outside the restaurant's picture window. This was the biggest fish I had ever seen, and it was an awesome, distracting sight. It was weird though because many people were moving about on the docks, but no one seemed to be giving the huge shark a second look. It was as if sights like this were common, and a fish of this size was simply no big deal. Well, it was a big freaking deal to me. It was an incredible animal, and there it was, not 20-ft from my burger and fries. I was starting to think that Montauk just might be my kind of town.

I wish I had a nickle for every photo taken of the Montauk Point Lighthouse.

After lunch we took a walk to check out the boats. Once on the docks, all the serious looking fishing vessels immediately mesmerized me. Most of the boats seemed to be similar in size and shape and had eye-catching, sweeping lines. To my eyes these boats seemed to be more beefy and rugged looking than the ones I was used to seeing on our home waters of the Western South Shore. Soaring masts, towers, and riggings were everywhere, and each boat seemed capable to safely wrestle with a mako similar in size to the one hanging over at West Lake Lodge. As I gazed at these salty looking vessels, I thought to myself, *someday...I have got to get one of these.*

We soon decided to head back to our room for a snooze before heading out with Captain Bob later that night. My brother has always been big on afternoon naps, and of course he fell out like a rock. Not me. I was simply too excited to doze off. So there I lie, staring at the ceiling, as the scent of the sea and sounds of the harbor enveloped me through the screened windows.

Around 8:00 P.M. my brother stirred and we both began getting ready for the night's expedition. We loaded our bags with sandwiches, and a few extra sweatshirts for the night chill. The last items we put in our bags were brand new rubber boots, and Helly Hansen bottoms. Bob had stressed to us how important these items were for comfort while out on the water at night.

We hopped into the car for the short ride to Gone Fishing Marina on East Lake Drive and we arrived just before 9:00 P.M. We gathered our gear, walked down the dock, and found Captain Bob getting his 24' *Rainbow* ready. Boy…was he ever raring to go. He hurried us aboard, and introduced himself to me. We also met his mate John Alberda at this time. Incidentally, Captain John Alberda was soon to become a legendary striper skipper in his own right. In fact, John ran his business for many years with a former boat of my brother's; a 28' Aquasport Family Fisherman. After introductions, we stowed our gear, donned our "rubbers" and in no time we were motoring our way out of Montauk Harbor.

The ride to the fishing grounds was awesome. The water was flat calm, and the quality of my night vision due to the full moon was amazing. As we cruised along, I could clearly see the sandy shore of Shagwong Point on the starboard bow, while on the port side the Inner Shagwong Buoy pulsed brightly in the night. The only audible sounds were the humming of the engine, and the swooshing of the hull as it skimmed over the water. This combo was like music to my ears. I was keyed up, but at the same time, it had been a long exciting day for me. So, while we ran towards the Point I took a seat facing the stern to watch John busily attaching sinkers, sharpening hooks, and hooking eels.

Once Captain Bob eased off on the throttle, I felt a renewed vigor envelop me. Bob had stopped way up-tide of the spot, so he had plenty of time to explain his technique. I listened intently, attempting to absorb every iota of this tutorial. Bob finished his spiel with something in the order of, "Okay, both John and I are going to fish and if we hook up we'll hand you the rod." I quickly chimed in, "No, you're not." In the bright moon glow I could clearly see a look of confusion and perhaps a bit of annoyance on Bob's face. So I chimed back, "No thanks," but quickly added, "Hey, you guys can fish all night, catch as many as you can, but if I don't hook it- I'm not catching it." Bob looked at me, smiled, and said, "Okay kid, you're on your own." He then turned to John and said, "Make sure you teach this kid the right way."

Bob and John worked their butts off trying to find fish. We drifted over every spot in Bob's list of "numbers," and even with Bob's superior knowledge none of us had a bite the entire night. Nonetheless, it was a great learning experience because Bob taught us many things, and answered all our questions about striped bass throughout the night. The fact that we didn't catch any striped bass was only a minor annoyance because we learned so much in the process.

It was indeed a long, long night. However, I never wanted it to end because I was now certain if anybody was going to get us into big bass it was going to be Captain Bob Rocchetta. Eventually, as a pink false dawn began to shimmer in the eastern sky, we gave up drifting live eels. I assumed Bob would be heading for the dock, but he must have felt really sorry for us because it was soon clear he had other intentions. At this point, we were almost 9-hours into the trip with not so much as a sniff or tap on any of our baits. Bob announced it was time to change tactics and try some diamond jigging for weakfish.

After a short run, Bob found a flock of diving birds, and we quickly proceeded to have a ball jigging up a mess of big weakfish, bluefish, and porgies. During the blitz, our attitudes must have

Me, Capt. Bob, and Pete with the mount of Bob's 76-pounder at a striper fishing seminar in the late 80's.

impressed Bob because from that point on a cherished friendship developed between us all. I guess while making a friend, we had inadvertently found the mentor we badly needed.

On another later trip, Captain Bob did get us our first large stripers, twin 30-pounders, caught trolling Danny Plugs in the rips off Block Island. Again, this experience took place under the "Shangri La of a summer moon." As you can imagine, my brother and I were ecstatic. True, we had only scratched the surface of striper

The morning after another long night of fishing, our first large stripers

Listen carefully, and you might here some background gunfire in this photo.

angling, but at least now we felt that we were heading in the right direction.

Shortly after our first couple of charters with Captain Bob, we began to heed his advice, and guess what? We started catching stripers. Fishing at night, drifting eels on the ebb tide, in the vicinity of East Rockaway Inlet became our forte. We never caught any real whoppers, but I cherish the memories of those trips because this is the time we began to tally some impressive striped bass catches all on our own. Incidentally, it was common on these nighttime excursions to hear "celebratory" gunfire coming from the Rockaway Housing Projects that were located nearby...nice!

In 1984 I was still working in Herman's and attending Queens College. At this point, I was just taking up "space" in school, and by no means was I going to be a rocket scientist. So it was time to get a real job. In the fall I took the test to become a New York City Police Officer, and by late 1985 I had completed all of the qualifying requirements. I was hoping to join the NYPD, but my civil service list number came up for the New York City Transit Police.

Let me digress to explain my feelings about this development. In High School I attended La Salle Academy located at 2nd Ave. and 2nd St. in Manhattan. On every school day I had to deal with a subway commute. Plainly put, this commute sucked, and the F-train 2nd Ave stop where I got off... sucked even more. In addition, the neighborhood above was best described as a hell hole. At the time, crack was whack, and heroin was sold openly. Whenever I stepped off the train at 2nd Ave skells, crack heads, and the skankiest prostitutes imaginable ruled the roost in this reeking subway station.

During one F-train ride I firmly decided that I never wanted a job that involved a subway commute. Now, on the verge of joining the New York City Police Department, I was being told I was going to be working in the subway on an everyday basis with the Transit Police. Naturally, I wasn't too keen on this prospect. Right there, as I was told to go "upstairs" and sign the paperwork for the Transit Police, I first found a pay phone to call my Uncle Frank Maciewski to relay my feelings. Uncle Frank was a retired NYPD detective and and had pushed me strongly to take the Police test in the first place. On that phone call he basically said, "Don't be stupid kid, take the job, and get the pension time rolling." Honestly, I really wasn't thinking about a pension at that stage of my life, but my parents had made it abundantly clear it was time to get a job with both benefits and security. I did not want to disappoint my parents or uncle just

because I hated the subway. So, I hung up the phone, and with slight trepidation, went upstairs to sign the paperwork to join the New York City Transit Police.

On January 9, 1986 I raised my right hand, and along with 2,500 other recruits we were all sworn in by the late Mayor Ed Koch as members of New York's various Law Enforcement Departments that at the time included the New York City, New York Transit, and New York Housing Police Departments.

July 1986 graduation from the NYPD Academy.

I graduated from the Police

Academy in the summer of that year and was assigned to District 4, located at 14 St. Union Square. Guess where my first tour of duty took place? You guessed it, that same smelly 2nd Ave subway station that I loathed from my La Salle days. Life certainly can throw some nasty ironies one's way, can't it?

Not all assignments were as crappy as 2nd Ave. and I eventually enjoyed being a Transit Police Officer. My finest times on the Department were the four years I spent in the Firearms Training Unit as an Instructor. In this unit, we specialized in transitioning the whole Transit Police Department from .38 revolvers to Glock .9mm semi-automatic pistols. This unit was made up of a great bunch of officers, and we had a lot of fun doing a very important job.

About half of the NYTPD Firearms Unit is in this photograph taken around 1993 at the Mitchell Field Range in Nassau County.

I stayed on the Transit Police until 1995 when Mayor Giuliani and Police Commissioner William Bratton merged the Transit, Housing, and NYPD into one Department. As a result, I did eventually make it onto the NYPD. But, I have another cruel irony about this development. Before the merge, I had studied my butt off and passed the Sergeant test. At the time of the merge I was 23-names away from being promoted, and that's basically an imminent promotion. In spite of this, the merge negated my current list number, and I was shifted to the rear end of the NYPD Sergeant list. Consequently, I never did get promoted from that list. In fact, in 1996 I had to take the Sergeant's test again. I passed it again, and eventually got promoted to Sergeant in July 1998. Incidentally, I actually passed the Sergeant's test three times in my career, and why I didn't get promoted the first time around is another whopper of irony, but that's a story for another time.

Elena and I outside 1 Police Plaza on the day of my promotion to Sergeant 1998.

Upon reaching my 20th year of service I was done in more ways than one, and in January 2006, I pulled the pin and retired. Retiring at 41-years of age was a very cool thing, and for that I'm ever grateful to my late Uncle Frank. Now, I'm not going to be one of those guys who gushes how much they loved being a cop on the NYPD. Don't get me wrong, being a cop had its moments, and I also enjoyed meeting and working with some great people. In fact, many of these same people are still my dear friends to this day. In spite of this, I despised the politics, nepotism, and B.S. that reigns within a huge organization like the NYPD. Add in all the second-guessing that comes from a clueless media and the job gets real old, real early in one's career. Therefore, I'd been planning my retirement, and my second career as a charter captain since about...oh let me think...1990, which was only four years after taking the job. In relation to this, in August 1993 I passed the United States Coast Guard Captain's test and received my Captain's license.

That first night striper trip with Captain Bob Rocchetta has had a long lasting effect on me. Bob treated us with great respect, and even though the striper fishing was disappointing, he was severely locked in, and worked like a man possessed trying to find us some stripers. I loved everything about the experience, but what especially hooked me was the freedom. After dealing with the Police Department for twenty years, freedom was clearly something I craved.

Yes, the liberation of being the boss is awesome. The sunset views from the captain's chair aren't too shabby either, and they sure beat the hell out of some the sights I was privy to while "on the job." The excitement felt aboard my boat when a big fish is landed is wonderful, and it's this "feeling" that constantly reassures me that I'm in the right place, at the right time of my life. I truly believe when the weather is right and the fish bite, I have the greatest job in the world.

In retrospect, it sure seems like I've come a long way from that Queens stoop when on a July night in 1981 I predicted, *someone is going to catch a big striper tonight.*

Welcome to my office.

Chapter 2

Getting One of These

Once I settled on becoming a full time charter boat captain upon retiring from the NYPD, it was eventually time to find the right boat that would let me specialize in catching striped bass. The profit margin is narrow in chartering, so buying a big sportfisherman with twin engines was out of the question because of cost and expenses. I have been on a number of different types of vessels over the years, and they all got the job done to some degree. However, a custom boat, built specifically to my needs as a striper angler, began to win favor in my mind. I required a boat that rode smoothly, was economical to run, and large enough to safely fish in lousy weather. My idea for the perfect striper boat was narrowed down in 1997, when my brother Pete purchased a 35' kit boat-Down-Easter from T-Jason Boats in Steuben, Maine.

The first time I saw the project in Pete's driveway I was stunned by the enormous undertaking of getting this boat fishable. There was nothing inside the hull except for the engine, main stringers, bulkhead, and fuel tanks. There was no decking, floor, windows, cabin, or…anything. I thought he was completely nuts, but he seemed to be reveling in his insanity.

A custom boat sounds great, but regardless of whether you build a custom boat from a kit, or have a builder finish it for you, the entire process is painfully slow because each boat is unique. Add the fact that most components have to be fiberglassed in place and allowed to cure before proceeding, and everything takes twice as long. However, Pete plowed happily along with his project. I helped where I could: grinding fiberglass here or gel coating there. Dealing with the fumes and fibers of building a fiberglass boat is an experience in itself because you are basically living in this smelly dusty environment for months on end. I can't tell you how much clothing I tossed in the trash when the project was over, but it was substantial, and I'm sure whatever I tossed away, my brother tripled.

Although the boat was not completed, eventually it was well enough along to be launched. The *Miss Mac* made its debut at Montauk in the late summer of 1998. On her first cruise I was immediately impressed by the smooth, non-pounding ride. The wind was blowing from the northwest at around 15-knots and the *Miss Mac* effortlessly ran at 17-knots, confidently slicing through tight 4-ft waves.

A recent photo of the Miss Mac *cruising easily off Montauk.*

Heading east from the harbor to the point was an easy run, but when we turned around to go back to the dock, I was really impressed. The boat sliced through the head seas, throwing sheets of spray up and over the pilothouse, like it was only a simple annoyance. This is when I discovered that Down-Easters have a wet ride when running straight into a stiff breeze, but this is why the boats are designed with an enclosed pilothouse. I just would not recommend working in the cockpit under such conditions because you are going to get pretty wet. The run back to the dock was sweet, and somewhere along Gin Beach I realized that my days in a 23' center console were quickly ebbing away.

Me and a 33-pound striper caught on my center console in Reynold's Channel.

Down-Easters have a cult following among many hard core anglers. However, some seem to have distorted views of what Down-Easters are designed to do. These boats are most stable and comfortable when their sharp bow and full keel remain in the water. In this position, the hull parts the waves like a hot knife through butter. Yes, I know all about the lobster boat races that take place in Maine where the boats roar along at insane speeds. However, take a close look at those boats while they are steaming at wide open throttle. The hulls are almost completely out of the water, and the purpose of the displacement hull and full keel is defeated, resulting in diminished stability.

It takes a lot of horsepower to get a 35' Down-Easter to run along at 30-knots, and I'd estimate 600-HP is needed. Increased horsepower means fuel consumption rises considerably. An important concept behind the Down-East hull design is the ability to use a single engine to establish a respectable cruising speed, and keep fuel consumption to a minimum. The *Miss Mac* has a 350 HP CAT, and it cruises between 15 to 17-knots while burning approximately 8-gallons an hour. In my opinion, these are great numbers for a charter fishing boat because whatever blows out the exhaust comes right out of the wallet.

I fished on the *Miss Mac* at Montauk for a number of seasons and after each trip it was harder for me to go back to my center console docked in Freeport. The reasons were two-fold; first, the ride and comfort of 35' boat, with a full pilothouse was very easy to get used to. I quickly began to realize that fishing on my boat during cold November days was no longer fun. Second, the fishing at Montauk is often outstanding and once catching 30 to 40-pound stripers and 5 to 8-pound fluke becomes a regularity, it's difficult to go back to Jones Inlet, and be satisfied with the fishing there. So, with my brother having a nice big boat at Montauk, I was being hit with a double whammy because I craved a bigger boat of my own, and I wanted to eventually dock it at Montauk.

A 48 and 38-pounder caught in back to back drifts on the Miss Mac.

In the fall of 2000, I approached my wife Elena and broached the subject of buying a bigger boat. By the way, I met my wonderful wife while working at Herman's World of Sporting Goods, in 1985. Since we've met, Elena has always been wonderful about my striper fishing obsession, and I am truly blessed to have her in my life. We have been married since 1991, and never once has she said to me, "You can't go fishing today." However, buying a bigger boat was definitely going to stretch the budget. Regardless, Elena did not flinch and said, "If you want a bigger boat, and we can afford it, get it".

Again, I'll reiterate, I am indeed a blessed person to have Elena as my wife and best friend.

A cute picture of Elena, and a crappy one of me with Elena's first striper at Montauk.

I knew I wanted a Down-Easter, but the questions were which one and how big? I talked this over with my brother, and with his guidance I started leaning towards a 30' boat. I was not sure whether I wanted a new or a used boat, but after looking at a few used models and seeing the ridiculous prices being asked for beat-up old lobster boats (Down-Easters) with tired engines, I decided new was the way to go. I began gathering literature from Maine builders such as Terry Jason, H&H, Young Brothers, General Marine, and Duffy/Atlantic Boats. I read their stat sheets with delight, but to be quite honest, terms like quarter guards, bronze bearings, wet keels, and cored hulls went right over my head. I realized I had to look into this project a little more deeply. As a result, I began to burn up the phone lines talking to various builders.

Pete had nothing but good things to say about his dealings with Terry Jason, who is a transplanted Long Islander. I met Terry on a trip to Maine that I made with Pete, and found him also to be a kind and honorable man. While chatting with Terry I discovered that one of his 28' boats was located on Shelter Island. So on a cold January day I set up a visit with the boat's owner. I took Pete along with me for the ride and advice. I knew the boat would be out of the water, and that would make a ride out of the question, but I was already confident in the ride of T-Jason boats.

Upon arrival, I was immediately impressed with the boat's classic lines. I spoke to the owner and quizzed him about running speed, fuel consumption, and whether or not he was happy with the boat. I took some pictures of the boat and soon we were on our way home.

I eventually settled on the T-Jason 28'. I called Terry up and we discussed final pricing. Soon a deposit check was sent. And yes, I questioned my sanity also because although the boat would be partially built to kit specifications, I was going to complete the rest of the build in Pete's Freeport driveway just like Pete had done with the *Miss Mac*.

The hull was scheduled to be delivered in August of 2002, and I really wanted it to arrive on schedule because I was hoping to get the decks glassed-in before winter. Well of course the boat was a little late and the hull arrived in October. Unfortunately, along with the boat came some nasty Maine weather, including an early snowfall. The rest of the autumn was unseasonably cold, and I never did get those decks down before the end of 2002.

The weather finally turned and I started working on the boat in earnest by March of 2003. The experience was a good one because I learned where every nut, bolt, and fitting was located. But damn, it was hard work. Luckily, my brother lives around the block from Fred Chall Marine because I must have made a couple hundred visits there during the construction. Pete and my friend Ed Caroselli helped me a lot, and after a few months things started to come together.

I had been kicking around boat names since the day I ordered the kit. It was a fun word game, and I had been scouring the dictionary and the Internet for worthy ideas. Originally the boat hull was going to be red, and I was pretty sold on the name

Above: Pete and I on delivery day of my T-Jason 28' kit boat in Freeport, NY.

Below: Ed Caroselli and I inside the pilothouse of my kit boat. Ed is standing where the cabin door would eventually be, and I'm at the future helm position.

Red October, but I eventually switched to a light blue hull, so Red October went into the garbage can. Other names I considered were Night Stalker, Midnight Rambler, Linesider, and High Liner. One night I was watching the James Bond classic "Goldfinger". About a quarter of the way through the movie Bond discovers Goldfinger's plan to rob Fort Knox was named Operation Grand Slam. This name immediately jumped out at me because a grand slam is a good thing in both baseball, (my favorite sport), and in fishing scenarios. So, *Grand Slam* was it.

I could see the light at the end of the tunnel for a launch date by June. The vessel was nowhere near complete, but I'd finished enough work so it could be put into the water and do some fishing. I had vacation the last two weeks of July, and during this span I worked 10-straight, 14-hour days to get the boat ready for a hull dunking. Most of the last few days involved marathon wiring sessions for electronics, pumps, and lighting. I had never done wiring, and believe it or not, upon launching, every one of my electronic connections worked. I was indeed pretty impressed with myself.

The first time I turned the key and the Yanmar rumbled to life, it was truly a hell of a kick. I piloted the *Grand Slam* from the marina, and slowly motored through the No Wake Zones in the area. All the while, I tentatively checked all systems to insure that everything was working up to snuff. Once I got free of the No Wake zones, I slowly pushed the throttle forward and the hull responded accordingly to the increased power. The engine was revved up to a cruising rate of 2800 RPMs, and this caused the craft to hum along at 19-knots. All systems continued to work fine, so I nailed the throttle to 3400 RPMs, and the boat growled down the channel at 25-knots. The rush I felt was fantastic, and suddenly all the time rolling around in fiberglass dust now seemed worth it.

I wanted to move my boat to Montauk someday, but at the time I purchased the 28' I was not sure when this was going to

Above: *Pete and I in the mostly finished pilot house of the original* Grand Slam.

Below: *The* Grand Slam *running at 20-knots in Jones Inlet.*

happen. I lived in East Meadow and the chore of driving 100-miles each way to use the boat was not one I relished. Soon, Nassau County turned a difficult decision into an easy one when the powers that be reassessed my property taxes and basically doubled them. That's when Elena and I decided to sell the house and move further east. Truthfully, I would have loved to move to Montauk, but I still had time left with the Police Department, and Elena really did not want to move that far from the city. Eventually, we found a house in mid Suffolk County with double the living space we had in East Meadow. I now had a 59-mile run to Montauk. Still long, but when done in the early morning, or late at night, the trip is manageable.

My 28' Grand Slam *cruising off Montauk Point.*

The move was made, and the following spring I moved the boat to Montauk. Unfortunately, I soon found out that the 28' was a little too small for the often-turbulent East End waters of Montauk. I was simply getting blown-out too frequently, especially during the productive fall months. And to be honest, the boat was a little crowded with five people onboard.

So, you guessed it, after just three seasons with the 28' *Grand Slam* I had to again approach Elena about buying a bigger boat. Once again to my eternal relief she said, "Go for it." Did I ever mention how lucky I am to have Elena as my wife?

The whole boat building process began anew. I was leaning

Me with the last striper caught on the original Grand Slam *December 06.*

towards a 40' Osmond-H&H, but when I discovered the amount of fuel I would be burning to get this vessel to cruise at 15 to 20-knots, I quickly lowered my expectations. The *Ginger-Al* is a 36' Osmond-H&H that is berthed next to the *Miss Mac* in Montauk. I loved the lines of this boat, and I began to seriously contemplate buying one of these.

Capt. Al Giglio's beautiful 36' Osmond -H&H Ginger-Al.

In October of 2006, Elena and I decided to take a ride up to

Maine to speak with the people at H&H, and while up there, since Terry Jason's place was just down the road, I also decided to meet with him, too. Now, I love Pete's boat, and I loved my 28' but honestly I was leaning towards the 36' Osmond-H&H.

Elena and I drove up to Maine on a Friday with our two dogs Lacey and Shelby. The H&H office was closed on the weekend, so we met with Terry at his place on Saturday and he treated us like family. After all, the Mikoleski's had already bought two boats from him, so everything was nice and comfortable. We soon got down to business and I laid out exactly what I wanted in my next boat.

My wish list consisted of the following: a cruising speed of at least 17-knots, bridge station, helm station, bunks for 3, head with a separate stalled shower, heat, A/C, tuna door, inverter, microwave, refrigerator, two sinks with fresh hot water, belt driven wash-down pump, insulated fish hold, adequate seating for 6, aluminum framed windows, and a winter back with a sliding door. Terry said all of this would fit in the boat no problem.

Me and Terry Jason discuss the 35' Grand Slam - October 2006.

On the ride back to our hotel, Elena and I were very comfortable with the notion of signing a contract with Terry Jason right then and there, and I had to push myself to at least hear what H&H had to offer.

On Monday we made the visit to H&H Boats and I was taken on a tour of the shops. The H&H set-up was much larger than Terry Jason's "mom and pop" operation. I was impressed with all the boats that were being built, and I was again reminded how much I liked their 36'. I presented my identical wish list to the office manager, and I was told it would take a few days for him to get back to me with a price. Well, a few days turned into about a month, and when the final figures of both projects arrived in the mail, the prices of the boats were very different. Terry Jason had easily won the "closed bidding" and in a few days a deposit check was on its way to Steuben, Maine for a Terry Jason 35' that would be powered by a 3126 420-HP Caterpillar diesel engine.

The first photo of my 35' Grand Slam. The hull and top are two separate pieces that are joined together - February 2007.

The hull was laid up during Christmas week of 2006. I soon made a few trips up to Maine while the "bones" of the vessel were built in order to watch Terry work on the hull. As one can imagine, the wait for the boat was excruciating. However, the build moved steadily on, and I made several visits to the shop to check on progress.

The *Grand Slam* was eventually delivered by truck to Mystic, Connecticut, and I finally got her into the water in August of 2007 for the steam to Montauk. My friends Erik Weingartner and Jack Fox were along for the ride that day, and of course, we had to make my first ever cruise from Mystic, with a new boat, and unfamiliar electronics, in dense fog. How wonderful! Thankfully, about 4-miles from Montauk Harbor the fog lifted, and I was able to tool up the throttle and ran the rest of the way home at 17-knots.

As of this writing I'm happily catching striped bass on the new *Grand Slam* at Montauk. The hull cruises nicely at 2200 RPMs in the 17-knot range and burns about 20-gallons of fuel per inshore fishing trip. The boat takes the nasty seas Montauk is famous for quite well, and my customers and I are very happy with the vessel. I foresee running my 35' T-Jason for many years to come. However, I'm sure the quest for a bigger boat will one day bite me again. I know the new 47' Osmond-H&H is a beast of a boat.

Oh Honey… can we have a little talk?

A 36-pound striper is landed on the Grand Slam.

Chapter 3

The Striped Bass

As a charter boat captain I have to be good at catching many kinds of fish. As stated, the fish that obsesses me is the striped bass. If you have a similar obsession, it's in your best interest to learn as much about this game fish as possible. With this in mind, let me introduce you to my "favorite" nemesis, the striped bass.

Imagine a "fish", and the beautiful profile of a striper should immediately conjure within your mind.

Striped bass are found mainly within the inshore waters between Maine and North Carolina. Stripers are a long-lived fish that can grow to very large sizes. They commonly reach 30-pounds, and each season 50-pounders are encountered by anglers, and occasionally larger specimens over 70-pounds are landed. The striper's ability to grow an impressive size is a major reason for their popularity among anglers. However, the fact that striped bass can be very tough to catch makes landing a large one a special experience. Stripers are also popular because they can be caught by a variety of means from bottom fishing with bait in a tranquil harbor, to casting an artificial lure in a pounding surf.

I never tire of admiring big stripers like this one.

Coming eye to eye with a real big striped bass is one of the greatest treats in the angling world. The really big ones are impressive brutes that will leave you awed by their power and guile. A 50-pounder held at chest level by an average sized man results in the tail of the fish still brushing the ground. The first time a big striper is hooked be prepared for a fight that stays down deep in the water column, with several strong runs the rule. This initial encounter is often enough to lead one on a life-long quest for the mighty striper.

Big striped bass always result in big smiles. Photo: Capt. Pete Mikoleski.

Striped bass have the scientific name of Morone saxatilis. Saxatilis translates to rock dweller, and anyone who has fished for stripers knows this is an accurate description. Stripers love rocks, more precisely, stripers love to feed on what lives around rocks. Their prey includes, but is not limited to crabs, lobsters, squid, eels, bergals, and blackfish. Striped bass also like rocks because they use them as blocking devices to avoid current flow. Stripers often lie behind a rock, conserve energy, and wait for prey to be pushed within striking distance. Striped bass seek rocks so often that in their southern range stripers are called rockfish. In other places along the coast they go by such colorful names as linesider, greenhead, pajama fish, and squid hound.

A 34-pound "Squid Hound" caught by Michael McDermott, assisted by Grand Slam *mate, Kenny Leon.*

The word used to describe large female striped bass is cow. These fish of 30-pounds and larger have sizeable heads with big eyes that are able to see prey superbly in turbid water, or on dark nights. Striped bass have two nostril holes on the top of their head that can detect baitfish 300-ft away. A striper's excellent eyesight, superior sense of smell, and the sonar capabilities of their lateral line combine to make them a supreme hunter.

The mouth of striped bass appears to contain no teeth, but a closer inspection reveals tiny teeth that have the consistency of rough, prickly, sandpaper. Also, within the striper's mouth are sensors that allow bass to taste and differentiate between varieties of substances. Always keep in mind, a striper doesn't chew its prey, it simply grabs and swallows it whole. Specimens of 20-pounds and larger have no problem swallowing 1 to 2-pound fish like a porgy or bunker.

A chunky "linesider" caught on a live lined scup that barely fit into the striper's mouth.

The body of a big bass is graced with thick shoulders and a girthing belly that streamlines into a torpedo shape ending in a large, fan-shaped tail. A striper's flanks are silvery with iridescent tones, and a series of prominent horizontal black stripes. The skin towards the underbelly gradually turns to a bright white. On top of the body are two dorsal fins. The forward dorsal contains 6 to 10-large rays that when erect are sharp as ice picks. The rear dorsal is slightly aft of the first, and this fin along with the bottom anal fin are more compact, and contains 10 to 13-softer fin rays. On each side of the body, just behind the gill plates are twin pectoral and lower caudal fins that enable the striper to make precise vertical and horizontal movements. The very top of a striper's back can range in color from light bronze to deep purple or black. The body is covered with armor-like scales, on larger specimens these scales can be almost 2-inches wide.

Striped bass that reach 15-years can exceed 40-pounds

in weight, and rarer 50-pounders are usually at least 20-years old. These older fish are females. Rarely do males live past 11-years of age, so when a striper larger than 34-inches is caught, chances are it's a female.

The mount of a big beautiful striped bass

How big do striped bass grow? In 1891 off North Carolina, a commercially caught fish tipped the scales at 125-pounds. In 1995, while conducting research, the Maryland Department of Natural Resources netted a 92-pounder. The current world all-tackle record is 81.8-pounds caught by Greg Myerson in August 2011. This massive bass inhaled a live eel drifted close to a large boulder off Westbrook, Ct. This huge bass took the IGFA crown away from the 78.8-pound striper that was caught off Atlantic City, NJ in September of 1982 by Albert McReynolds.

Striped bass range from Canada to Florida, and there is also a limited number of striped bass found in the Gulf of Mexico and the Mississippi River. Striped bass are a hardy fish that can manage to thrive in conditions that are often considered far from ideal by human standards. Striped bass are great at adapting. In 1881, 435-small stripers were transported via huge water tanks on a train from New Jersey to California. At that time no striped bass lived on the west coast. These stripers were released into the waters of San Francisco Bay. Twenty years later the commercial west coast landings of stripers reached 1,234,000 pounds.

Striped bass are an anadromous fish. This means they spend most of their life in saltwater, and like salmon, return to the freshwater rivers to spawn. Because of this characteristic they have flourished after being released in many land-locked lakes and reservoirs throughout the United States. These fresh water impoundments have little current flow, and current is crucial for a natural successful spawn. In order to keep these populations healthy, annual stocking is required. But stripers continue to grow as they live, and on February 28, 2013 James Bramlett landed a 70-pound fresh water striper in the Black Warrior River of Alabama. This fish was only 45.50 inches long, but had a girth of 37.75-inches, and is a pending world record for landlocked striped bass.

The important spawning estuaries on the east coast include the Chesapeake Bay and Hudson, Delaware, and Roanoke Rivers. In these estuaries, the conditions are similar and spawning occurs from March to May when water temperatures are between 58 to 64-degrees.

Female striper's become sexually mature between ages 4 and 8, while males become mature between ages 2 and 3. It is believed that females give off a scent signaling their ripeness and this encourages the males to follow them up-river to the spawning grounds. Female bass seek out areas with current that help keep the eggs buoyant after release. When eggs are released in stagnant water, most fall to the bottom and suffocate in the silt.

When a male, or group of males, sense that a female is ready to release her eggs they will begin to prod and butt her belly. This pushes the spawning event to the surface and results in a commotion that southern anglers call a "rock fight". Once a female releases hers eggs, males swim through them releasing milt to fertilize the eggs.

Female striped bass become sexually mature when they reach

between 21 to 31-inches in length, and weigh between 6 to 15-pounds. Females in this size range release about 500,000 eggs annually. Research over the last two decades has indicated that females in this size range are responsible for the majority of the egg production during the spawn. A big striper of 40-pounds or larger produces more than 3,000,000 eggs when she spawns, but consistent spawning seasons are now behind her in this size range. However, according to Byron Young, former Chief of NYS DEC Finfish and Shellfish, when a bass over 40-pounds does spawn, the eggs are bigger and more viable, and more of her eggs are likely to hatch.

Stripers, like this 26-pounder, are consistent spawners in the prime of their live's, and can be counted on to add millions of eggs to the annual spawn for several more seasons.

Even though big cows only spawn sporadically, I firmly believe we should try to release many of the larger sized striped bass we catch. These big fish have been running the coastal gauntlet for close to 20-years, and I feel in my heart that these impressive specimens have earned a "senior rank." These big bass also carry genes for larger size, and when they do spawn this trait can be passed along to their offspring.

Once the eggs are fertilized they hatch within 29 to 80-hours. Newly hatched striped bass larvae live off their egg yolk sacks for 5-days while their bodies develop. When this period is over, they begin feeding on zooplankton that consists of microscopic crustaceans and insect larvae. If the right organisms are not available for food during this critical time of their development, many of the fry will die. The fry feed voraciously, and before long they will take on the shape and markings of adult stripers. Most young of the year striped bass will stay within the river of their birth until 2-years of age and approximately 14-inches in length before joining the annual migration.

This husky striper, caught in early October at Montauk ,was on it's "Fall Run" to Southern waters.

After spawning, most of the Chesapeake stripers will head north to spend a good part of the year in the waters of the mid Atlantic and New England states. The Hudson fish travel a little less, as they are rarely found south of New Jersey, or north of Massachusetts. Traditionally, by the second spring moon period in June, the big stripers are on station in various fishing hot spots up and down the striper coast.

Stripers aren't picky eaters. Common sense dictates if a fish has the genetic ability to grow larger than 100-pounds, they simply can't be fussy. But, don't make the mistake of thinking striped bass are easy targets that will eat anything. Stripers can be cautious, selective, and lazy. To boot, they can be all these qualities at the same damn time.

Stripers like this feisty mid-thirty pound specimen are prolific eaters, but they can also be frustratingly picky at times, and be tough to fool into taking a bait.

Summer water temperatures will climb above 70-degrees, this is when stripers will become a little less aggressive, and seek deeper cooler water to feed. However, they are not against raiding the shallows for an easy meal under the cover of darkness. In September, the sun's rays become less direct and days also become shorter. This causes ocean and bay waters to slowly cool. Stripers will soon begin feeding heavily, and it is now time for them to start fattening up for the long journey back towards their spawning waters. This is the fall run and this is the time of the best striper angling in the Northeast.

The Chesapeake stock of stripers that summer in New England waters will usually be the first to move. Many of these schools will stop at Montauk Point, NY, and they use the strong currents found there to feed heavily on abundant shoals of baitfish. This intense feeding peaks between mid-September and late October. When these stripers move on, some fish will hug the South Shore of Long Island, and when this occurs surf casters enjoy solid action. Stripers almost always follow the bait, and many times the bait will wander out to depths of 70-ft or more, and close on their tails will be stripers.

A husky striper landed by Glenn Carr in the Midway Rips during Montauk's famed "Fall Run."

During the fall run the Chesapeake stripers will steadily move south, and once they reach the bait filled waters off North Carolina, they remain there during the winter months. Recently, the winter sport fishery in the ocean waters off Virginia and North Carolina has exploded with popularity. In January 2008, a new Virginia state record striper was landed by Fred Barnes that weighed 73-pounds. This record is not going to be on the books very long because in January 2012, a new pending Virginia state record was landed by Capt. Tim Cannon that weighed 74-pounds. The practice of harvesting a large number of these big fish at this time has sparked some controversy because the fish are so vulnerable. The Atlantic States Marine Fishery Committee has indicated the need for a discussion that could change future striped bass management regulations in order to help protect pre-spawn wintering stripers.

The Hudson stock of stripers begins leaving the waters of New England and eastern Long Island by mid-November. Some of these bass will prowl the South Shore of Long Island, but most will take a northern route into Long Island Sound. Recent research indicates a majority of the Hudson stock winters over in deeper sections of mid-Long Island Sound where they feed on bottom hugging mollusks and crustaceans. In March and April the Hudson stock begin to feel the spawning urge and start to move towards the Hudson River. Once

My brother Pete leads a Hudson River striper to the net.

in the Hudson, much of the spring striper spawn takes place between Poughkeepsie and Albany mostly during May. By the end of May the Hudson fish move down river and fan out in the bays, sounds, and ocean waters from New Jersey to Massachusetts.

Limited striped bass spawning also occurs in other rivers such as the St. Lawrence, Kennebec, Connecticut, Potomac, Brandywine, Delaware, and St. John rivers. There is also a Nova Scotia stock of stripers that spawns each June in the Gulf of Maine. The different striped bass stocks do occasionally mix. This could be accidental, but more than likely this is an evolutionary mechanism that helps maintain genetic diversity.

As a sport fishing angler I believe everyone along the coast should have access to catching striped bass. That said, harvesting stripers as they are "ripe" and ready to spawn just doesn't seem consistent with keeping the overall population of stripers strong. In Maryland, in the area of the Susquehanna Flats, there is a "catch and release only" striper season that runs from March to May. In relation,

Capt. Erik Weingartner prepares to release a bass to live and breed another day.

I feel more "catch and release only" areas should be established during the spring to allow more stripers to successfully spawn. Most true sport anglers will see the logic behind my thoughts about protecting the spawning stripers in order to help keep the striper population in tip-top shape. I also suspect that many anglers who prowl these same striper spawning grounds will disagree strongly with me. However, sometimes…the truth hurts.

John Modica with a healthy "squid hound" caught and released on the Grand Slam.

Chapter 4

The Striper's Place in History

Striped bass have played a fascinating role in the history of the Atlantic Coast, and it is a story that illustrates how entwined striped bass and America has been. It is an incredible story that will help you respect the striped bass even more.

The first written account of striped bass was from explorer John Smith who wrote in his journal dated 1614, "I myself at the turning of the tyde have seen such multitudes pass out of a pounce that it seemed to me that one might go over their backs drishod." In modern English, John was saying there were so many stripers in the fish traps that you could walk on their backs to cross a channel and not even get your feet wet. The early abundance suggests that striped bass were a main part of the diet of Pilgrims in the Massachusetts Bay Colony. In fact, one can imply that the first Thanksgiving dinner probably saw more striped bass consumed than turkey.

However, there is another dark side to this abundance. In 1634 striped bass were so abundant that many Pilgrims began using striper carcasses to fertilize their farming fields. When officials became aware of and a proclamation was quickly issued forbidding such wanton waste of these valuable fish. The regulation became the New World's first conservation law.

By the early 1800's sport fishing for stripers with cotton or linen hand lines and crude hooks fashioned from thin pieces of metal became popular. The bait of choice was usually a piece of lobster tail, bunker, or shucked clam. An angler would coil the casting line neatly in one hand and twirl the bait around their head until enough torque was generated for a decent cast. There were so many bass at the time it often did not take long for a tug to be felt at the end of the fishermen's line.

Angling from a boat was not common in the 1800's and most people fished from the shore. Soon inventive anglers began to cast artificial lures instead of bait. The first lures were called block tins. They were tear dropped shaped pieces of metal with a fixed hook. To improve the shiny appearance of these lures that quickly tarnished in saltwater, an angler would shine them by rubbing with sand. A popular size was 6-ounces and most shore fisherman used about 120-ft of linen line. The line would be lobbed into the water and the angler would quickly retrieve the lure back to shore. This method became known as "squidding", a term that is still used today to describe an angling technique with a diamond jig. Some of the more experienced casters would add a piece of striped bass belly or lobster tail to the hook on the tin to make the lure more appealing. Sometimes, in addition to casting and retrieving, the angler would walk or jog down the beach in order to "troll" the surf line.

By the late 1800's, trolling in the rips around Manhattan Island became a popular way to catch stripers. This would usually require a fisherman and an oarsman, who would also act as a gaffer once a fish was fought to the boat. Whole rigged squid was often the bait of choice, and though most of the fishing was still being done with hand lines, it was during this period that those who could afford it began using bamboo rods and revolving reel spools.

Around this time more people who lived along the coast began to fish both for sport and food. Soon, an interesting fishing culture developed and spread from New York to Massachusetts. Wealthy white collar industrialists and politicians from New York, Philadelphia, and Boston began opening and operating private striped bass clubs. The first of these clubs was launched from the famous New York City hotel, The St. James. It wasn't long before great parcels of seaside land were secured by these wealthy men to build grand clubhouses to pursue the striped bass in comfort and style.

The club regulars quickly discovered that stripers preferred to feed in the vicinity of rocky outcroppings with strong currents. Therefore, members commissioned the construction of fishing stands out on to the rocks near the rips. Granite boulders were drilled to accept iron pipe platforms to which a high wooden deck would be attached. Fighting chairs were placed at the end of the rustic piers where anglers could fight fish in relative safety. Of course, as with all fishing spots, the prime times to fish a particular spot were constantly changing through the course of a season. For fairness, members of the club were all assigned their spots by lottery, and each night a drawing was held to decide the positions for the next day's fishing. However, many times the better spots were automatically given to distinguished guests.

Locals, who became known as chummers, would be assigned to each platform and their days started long before the anglers because it was the chummer's job to procure the needed bait for the day's fishing. Chummers seeded the water in front of the platform with lobsters, bunker, and clams. Usually stripers were in a feeding frenzy by the time anglers arrived to fish. The chummers would also bait hooks and cast out the offering with the lumbering tackle of the time, but strict rules of the club prohibited them from fighting the fish. When a hooked bass was close enough to land, the chummer's job was to capture the fish.

One of the most famous of these clubs was the Cuttyhunk Club that was formed in 1865 on the extremely fertile striper shores around Cuttyhunk Island. To this day, these famed striper waters have produced a colossal number of huge stripers for the anglers who fish these waters. If you were to visit Cuttyhunk today, you'd still find rusted holes in various rocky outcroppings that once hosted the fishing platforms. In fact, the sprawling clubhouse is still present, and is now operated as a Bed and Breakfast. Oh, if those walls could talk they would be rife with bass tales that would make the skin of any striper nut crawl with envy.

The clubs remained popular as long as the striped bass fishing remained good. However, this was about to end with the turn of the century when industrialization around the striper breeding grounds slowly began destroying the fishery. It is quite ironic that some of these wealthy men, who cherished fishing for stripers, were probably affecting them the most via industrial pollution from their coastal companies. By 1907 the fishing was so poor that the Cuttyhunk Club was disbanded and the property sold.

Man made pollutants do make things tough for a species like the striped bass, but stripers are also a naturally cyclic species. To probe these boom and bust year's scientists got more involved with the fishery. The principal striped bass scientist of the mid 1930's was Dr. Daniel Merriman, who worked for the Oceanographic Laboratory of Yale University. Dr. Merriman recommended that the size limit for stripers taken in New York waters be raised from 14 to 16-inches. At that time, it was wrongly believed that most female stripers were sexually mature at this size. Regardless of this early error, the size limit remained 14-inches in the Chesapeake Bay, where half the commercial catch of striped bass for the entire East Coast occurred. On the prime fishing grounds further up in the bay, where the majority of the spawning occurred, Merriman recommended the size of 12-inches. Consequently, a great majority of stripers were simply harvested before they even had a chance to spawn, and clearly this would end up being a recipe for disaster.

In the late 1940's, the number of sport fisherman grew by leaps and bounds. A booming economy developed that provided men with more money and leisure time to pursue hobbies. About this time, spinning reels became widely available in the U.S. and made casting easier. These new fisherman quickly fell in love with the hard fighting and good-eating stripers. Pressure on the stripers increased so much that in 1945 Massachusetts quickly banned the commercial netting of stripers. Politicians rightly saw more votes in their constituencies based on the expanding numbers of sport fisherman, compared to the thin ranks of commercial fisherman. However, hook and line commercial fishing for stripers continues to this day in Massachusetts.

Currently, New York's licensed commercial fisherman receive 200-plus striped bass tags each season, and are allowed to keep stripers from 24 to 36-inches -July 1, to Dec. 15.

Commercial fishermen, being ever-resourceful, simply began fishing with hook and line to garner their catch, and this gave birth to the term "pin hookers". At this point a great blurring of the fishery occurred as many sport fisherman realized they could make a quick buck by selling their catch, and this led to an explosion of unregulated commercial fishing, that had more so-called sport fisherman in it than hard-core commercial fisherman.

From the 1960's to the 1980's striped bass were fished hard with ineffectual regulations that did not include daily bag limits. In addition, it was rare for a legal striper to be released. Fishing pressure was destined to catch up with the striped bass. However, what really hit the striped bass stock hard was the fact that during the 1970's the Chesapeake strain of striped bass was having great difficulties spawning successfully. The root of this problem was eventually found to be caused by run-off from farm pesticides and fertilizers that were polluting the nursery grounds of the young stripers. By the mid 1980's it was evident that drastic measures would be needed in order to save the striped bass. Thankfully, as you will see in the next chapter, fishery managers were able to get it right.

Chapter 5

The Stripers Return

I would like to stress that the good striped bass fishing we have had recently is a miracle compared to how lousy it was just a short time ago. The fishery in the 1980's was in dismal shape and this was a very tough time to learn how to catch stripers. In fact, I went years without hooking a single striper. In retrospect, this is probably the main reason why I'm so obsessed with them.

The collapse of the striper fishery began to make headlines, and in 1981 Congress passed legislation that created the Atlantic Striped Bass Conservation Act. It was this stroke of the pen that gave managers from the Atlantic States Marine Fishery Commission the power to install regulations that would eventually bring the stripers roaring back.

A striper fishery with a high percentage of big fish is not a healthy population, nor is one that has only small fish. What fishery managers are aiming for is a population of fish that spans the gamut of sizes of sexually mature specimens. To help, we can do our part by ensuring that laws like the Clean Water Act of 1984 are continually enforced. Laws such as this will give the stripers and other anadromous fish species their best chance to spawn in clean productive water. We also must limit the harvesting of the brood stock so that sufficient fish remain in the fishery to support good fishing.

In 1973, the commercial catch of striped bass exceeded 14.7 million pounds of fish coast-wide, but just 10-years later this number crashed to 1.7 million pounds. In 1979, Congressman Gary Studds, after reading the book *Striper*, by John Cole felt compelled to do something about the decline of the striped bass. The outcome was the "Emergency Striped Bass Research Study." This study discovered that habitat improvement and hatchery programs, along with public awareness of the problem, would be needed to save the striper. However, the most important step that saved the striped bass occurred when a moratorium on the harvesting of striped bass was put in place coastwide between 1984 and 1990.

The moratorium was ordered for several reasons. Chiefly among them were poor year classes. The Juvenile Striped Bass Survey has been done every year since 1954. The main goal of this survey is to document the annual year-class spawning success for the young of the year, YOY for short. In the early 1980's these results showed very poor recruitment, and managers felt something had to be done in order to reverse this trend.

The survey is made at 22-fixed stations divided among four of the major spawning and nursery areas within the Chesapeake Bay. Sampling is done monthly during July, August, and September. Haul seines are done a minimum of 30-minutes apart at each site. 132-samples are used to calculate a bay-wide average. The number of stripers captured in each haul are quickly counted, measured, and released. The numbers are processed and in October of each year the preliminary results are published.

As of 1984, the highest YOY index ever recorded (30) occurred in 1970. In 2012, the record low (0.9) was recorded. According to Maryland DNR Striped Bass Survey Leader Eric Durell, this record low was the result of a warm winter and dry spring, both these conditions are unfavorable for fish that return to freshwater for spawning.

In 1982 the YOY index hit an (8), and this was considered historically to be an average year, but this was the first average year since 1978. Managers quickly decided that the 1982 year class would have to be protected in order for the stripers to be given a chance at recovery. Protecting the 1982 year class laid the foundation for the recovery of the striped bass.

In 1989, the 1982 year class turned 7-years old, and most of the females were sexually mature. When the 1989 YOY index was published in October it revealed a YOY of (25), and this number allowed striped bass managers to judge the moratorium a success. The 1989 YOY was so good the average was raised from (8) to (11.9).

Me, Capt. Bob, and my buddy Capt. Wayne Hermann with Montauk stripers caught shortly after the moratorium was lifted.

What has become of the protected year class of 1982? In 2003, the 1982 year class fish reached 21-years of age, and that season many 50-pound striped bass were caught up and down the coast. In 2011, the first 80-pound striped bass was landed on rod and reel and it is a good bet that this fish was close to 30-years old, and it very well could have come from the spawns of the 1982 year class.

From 1993 to 2001 YOY indexes included several good year

classes that bested the (11.9) long term average. In 2003, it was estimated that the stock of stripers running the coast was in excess of 60-million fish.

What a trip! The stripers were back, and I got to spend the night catching them with my brother Pete, and dear friends Wayne Hermann, Phil Rizzo, and Capt. Bob.

The low YOY numbers of the early 80's were a big reason for the moratorium of 1984. However, other factors pushed managers to enact the moratorium. Chiefly among them were the high PCB counts found in many sampled fish. PCB's are toxic chemicals that cause diseases in humans and can be found in the sediment on the bottom of both the Hudson River and Chesapeake Bays. PCB levels in sampled stripers have been falling since the 1980's mainly because The Clean Water Act of 1984 reduced the amount of these chemicals in our waterways. Regardless of the falling levels of PCB's, the Maryland Department of Natural Resources recommends that the consumption of stripers be limited, and it is best to eat smaller fish because younger fish have lower PCB levels. When preparing stripers for consumption, the Maryland DNR also recommends removing the darker, reddish meat from the fillets because this is where the majority of the PCB's collect in the fish.

With the great comeback of striped bass now history, are we clearly on the right page of proper striper management? This is a tough question to answer because each season sport and commercial fishermen do remove a large portion of striped bass from the population. Consistently successful fishery management will always be difficult. In spite of this, there has to be a sweet spot that allows all parties to remove an amount of fish from the stock that still leaves enough fish in the population to insure quality fishing and long term success.

From 2004 to 2010, the estimated population of 67.5-million fish had declined to about 42.3-million fish. This decline results in smaller schools, and fewer schools, that cause stripers to avoid many inshore areas where anglers traditionally caught lots of them. Could the fishery be in trouble just 8-years after the population reached over 60-million fish? In recent seasons, New York and New Jersey are still experiencing good action, but there are storm clouds on the horizon that must be kept on the radar screen. In 2003, when the striper population was thriving, Maine, which is on the northern edge of the striper's range, was the scene of great catches of striped bass. Now, Maine is experiencing several very poor fishing years. This is a clear sign that the striper population is contracting.

The Chesapeake Bay Region is responsible for producing about 70% of the entire East Coast population of striped bass, but not all striped bass leave the Chesapeake Bay on an annual migration. For those bass that live in the bay year-round, studies indicate there may not be enough nourishment to sustain normal growth and health. In fact, studies done by the Horn Point Laboratory indicated that typical tissue from a healthy striped bass should be 70 to 74% water, 20 to 24% protein, and 2.5% fat. In 1998 and 1999, striped bass tissues were found to be made up of 80% water, 19% protein, and 0.5% fat. This strongly suggests that some stripers are nutritionally challenged.

There is also a chance that less food in Chesapeake Bay is compromising their immune systems. Many fish have contracted a disease called "Mycobacteriosis" that was at one time called fish tuberculosis and was discovered in the Philadelphia Aquarium in 1926. The present disease seems to be a little different because it is caused by a bacterium called Mycobacterium shottsii that was not discovered until 2001 by the Virginia Institute of Marine Science.

In some studies it has been found to infect half the fish that were sampled from the Chesapeake Bay. Some of the stripers with the disease have visible sores and ulcers; others appear to be abnormally thin. Dissection of infected bass reveals that the striper's organs are covered with ugly granular growths. It is not believed that these infected bass are a threat to humans and proper cooking should kill the bacteria. The disease can cause a skin rash called "fish handler's disease" for those who handle them. People handling these diseased fish are advised to wear rubber gloves and to wash their hands in a disinfectant soap after coming in contact with them.

Striped bass must eat to live, and they will adjust their diet to many types of food. It is a sure bet that stripers are now feeding more heavily on other species such as alewife, shad, spearing, croaker, and crustaceans like the blue claw crab. There are now new bunker regulations in place that limit the harvest of this baitfish within the Chesapeake Bay. This can only be a good thing for the stripers overall nutritional health.

Striped bass have shown again and again that when given half a chance they can remain prosperous. In today's world, we have the intelligence and technology to properly manage the striped bass, and it is our responsibility as stewards of the sea to ensure the health of this important fishery.

It doesn't only take huge stripers to bring out the smiles. Bass of all sizes are simply crowd pleaser's.

A thriving striper population, where bass are readily available along the coast, is a good thing for anglers. In relation, there are also many other people and businesses that are on the periphery of the striper fishery that also see benefits when striped bass are flourishing. More stripers equal more people fishing for them and this means more money being spent by anglers. This bolsters local communities where stripers are caught. I'm not only talking about party boats, charter boats, and tackle stores, but also marinas, gas stations, delis, restaurants, and hotels. When the economy is booming, life is good. So when the striper population is booming, how can this not be good for everyone?

Striped bass are more popular with sport anglers than ever before. The reason for this is because many other species of fish such as weakfish, whiting, flounder, and inshore tunas are almost non-existent catches for many fishermen nowadays. In order to bend their rods many anglers who once fished for other species have switched to striped bass fishing.

The Fall Run at Montauk is still productive, but in my opinion, it's not as good as it was just a few short seasons ago.

In my opinion, recently the number of striped bass in Montauk waters has been shrinking. This has been especially evident during the fall run. The last few falls the big striped bass have left by the end of October, and in November the fishing gets picky with smaller fish in the 24 to 32-inch range being the norm. Could this be a natural progression where big stripers migrate earlier with the majority of baitfish? Possibly, but I feel the steep decline from peak abundance in 2004 seems most likely to be culprit.

Yes, there is still a lot of striped bass swimming in Atlantic waters and I don't feel the stock is in danger of collapsing…yet. However, we must avoid the collapse of the fishery that occurred in the 80's. A return to those bleak days could destroy recreational fishing as we now know it in the Northeast. Currently there are triggers in place within the management system to help avoid such a collapse. I hope to the depth of my soul that such fail safe provisions will be enough to insure that the striped bass population remains in good shape for future generations of anglers.

Every angler who fishes for stripers cherishes a sight like this.

Chapter 6

My First 50

The 50-pound striper has been the Holy Grail for anglers who pursue this game fish. I have been fishing for striped bass since the 1970's, and as of 2008 I had not caught a 50-pounder. Honestly, this nagged at me, and the reason was simple. Ironically, the more successful my charter business becomes, the less I actually get to hold a rod. I'm on the water more than ever before, but I get to fish less, and that sucks. So, the lack of a 50-pounder was a monkey on my back that I wanted gone.

On October 9, 2008 I had arranged to take my cousin Mike Wesolowski and a few friends striper fishing. We were scheduled to meet at 2:00 PM at Montauk to fish the afternoon flood tide. The guys arrived late because of an auto accident in the Hamptons, so by the time they hopped aboard I was chomping at the bit. The ride to the point was nice and smooth. On the way, we passed schools of bluefish chasing bait to the surface, and I could sense some of my crew wanted to stop and fish at this surface feeding activity. In spite of this, I steamed on because it's been my experience that big bass do not usually take part in these surface-feeding frenzies, and I was pretty certain that there were some big stripers waiting for us in the rips off the lighthouse.

Soon, we passed Pollock Rip and the plotter indicated we were a half-mile from my targeted spot at the Elbow. I throttled back and told everyone to bait up, and soon I could hear eels being whacked against the transom.

I placed the boat on my numbers and told the guys to let their lines down. Conditions were perfect as we began our first drift.

The current was running at about 2-knots and light winds from the southwest were allowing us to drift directly north. No more than a minute into the drift, I turned to see Bob straining under the weight of a good fish. I instructed everyone to get their lines out of the water to avoid tangles with the hooked fish. Bob was excited and I did my best to talk him through the fight successfully. Bob had his hands full for a few minutes, but eventually steady pressure began to tire the striper. The striper took one final run at the boat before it was ready to be landed. I deftly netted the striper, and we had our first fish of the trip, a 25-pounder, on the deck.

Bob with the first fish of the trip.

I positioned us for the next drift and once the lines went down my cousin Mike hooked up almost immediately. Mike is an excellent angler, so I stayed silent, and admired the power of the striper. Soon a bigger bass in the thirties was in the boat. Another drift, another fish, and it was clear we were in the middle of a striped bass blitz.

Eventually, my hands began to itch for some action. The guys were doing very well, and I couldn't stand by any longer without getting a rod in the water. I went into the cabin and grabbed my custom made Lamiglas rod. I baited up, and nudged my way into a spot at the rail. I free-spooled the rig, letting the 10-ounce sinker touch down for a split second, and then cranked up 3-turns on the reel handle. About 200-ft into the drift I felt the tap, tap of a striking striper. I immediately dropped my rod tip towards the water and waited for the line to come tight. When the line tightened, I reared back on the rod to set the hook into the bulk of a nice striper. I said, "I'm in, anyone want it?" Rick was first to chime in. "I'll take it" and quickly we exchanged rods with each other. Rick fought the fish and in a few minutes he was leading another good bass into the landing net.

The bites kept coming.

On the next drift I was more intent on hooking and catching a striper, but I noticed Rick had held onto my custom rod. I guess he felt it was now a lucky rod. Luck seems to be a common feeling with superstitious anglers. I believe luck, especially when striper fishing, is baloney. But, on previous trips, Rick has been known to be "fish repellent." I thought, *no matter, my skills will out do Rick's bad mojo.* So, I took the rod he was previously using, which was one of my boat rods, and began fishing with it.

The action continued over the next few drifts and we began releasing some quality bass. However, the bites had stopped cold for me ever since I let Rick use my rod. I began to wonder if there was something to Rick's bad mojo after all, and that he had somehow managed to put a whopper of spell onto the rod I was now using.

The action at the Elbow eventually petered out so I announced, "If you guys are done playing with these small fish I'd like to move a little east to where the big girls live." The responses I received from the guys were, "Yeah right, whatever you say, Cap," and I might have heard, "He's full of crap," but I'm not sure.

After a short move, I signaled lines in. I grabbed "Rick's" rod, but before dropping down I wanted to change the eel. So I reached into a different bucket that contained dead eels "fresh," from my freezer. I wrap my eels in newspaper before freezing them, so they lie straight, and the eel I chose was a long fatty, that still had newspaper stuck to it. I peeled most of the paper off, but some shards remained. I wanted in on the drift, so I thought, *screw it,* and sent the rig to the bottom.

Seconds after dropping my newspaper enhanced eel into the drift I felt a hit. I reacted, dropping my rod tip towards the water, waited, and when the slack came out, I set the hook. The striper immediately made a strong run and peeled off a decent amount of line in the process. I have no idea how much line was taken, but the run lasted about 15-seconds. I knew my drag was set properly, and for a bass to take that much line, I felt this was a really good one.

This run stopped and I went to work getting line back onto the reel. I was able to gain some line, but this lasted only a few seconds before the bass tore off on another powerful run. Big bass normally take a couple of good runs, but usually each run is shorter than the last. Not this time. This second run was longer and stronger than the first. As line disappeared from the reel I thought, *this is a very good fish, don't screw it up!*

The run stopped eventually, and I noticed my line was beginning to take an angle indicting the fish was rising in the water column. I have no idea why the striper chose this tactic, but it was good with me. I have lost many big bass in the past because they stayed down deep, and they gained their freedom when the main line was cut by some underwater structure. If this striper wanted to fight near the surface, fine by me.

I pumped the rod smoothly, and reeled in line slowly, avoiding jarring actions that might cause the fish to shake her head, and throw the hook. On the next pump, I gained no line as the

Boat side acrobatics always keep the fight interesting when there is a big striper on the line.

reel's drag gave way in deference to the girth of a very big fish. I thought, *Okay, let's try that again.* Once again I pumped the rod and once again I lost line to the fish. The fight was now getting very interesting. Immediately, the idea of short-stroking came to mind. I have no idea why this notion popped into my head, but it was worth a try because I knew the longer the fight, the worse my odds were at winning.

I lifted the rod 5-inches, and reeled in fast as I lowered the rod tip. It worked. So I did it again… and again… and again. The striper reacted abruptly to this tactic and bolted towards the boat. I now reeled like a mad man to fend off any slack in my line. In a loud "swoosh", the bass broke the surface 50-ft off the port stern, and glided on the surface for a few seconds, with her large dorsal fin gracefully slicing through the calm water. Then, in a flash, she dove, disappearing in a shower of spray, leaving a hole in the water where she had just been.

This third run was much shorter and I could sense the time for landing the fish was near. I asked for the net. Instantly, with net in hand, Tom slid next to me at the port quarter. The striper popped to the surface again, this time only 10-ft from the boat. This closer look revealed I now had a 50-pounder within netting distance.

There was a 5-ft leader running to the hook, so I stepped back towards the starboard side to pull the fish within netting range. At this point, I lost sight of the fish and all I could do was hope that Tom would successfully net the fish. I knew we had the fish when Mike and Tom both bent over the transom to help hoist the heavy net basket into the boat.

There she laid a mass of muscle and girth. Finally, after all the years in pursuit of this trophy, I'd done it! My mind immediately flushed with a shower of thoughts. I wished my brother Pete was on board to share the glory. I also thought of all the advice from

The angle of the photo is horrible, but this is the first shot of my 54-pound striper.

Capt. Bob Rocchetta throughout the years. Finally, I thought of my Dad calling me and Pete "cuckoo" all those years ago. I was sure he was smiling at me now, and if he was there, he certainly would have blurted out something like, "Holy crap… that's a big friggin fish."

Finally!

We took a bunch of pictures, but out of the forty taken, only half were useful. I had a tape measure aboard and I measured the length at 52-inches, and the girth at 29-½-inches. I knew these measurements put the fish in the 50-pound range. Once things calmed down, I grabbed an old hand scale and put the bass on it. The needle stopped at 44-pounds. I thought, *What the…can't be?* I grabbed another scale, a lipper combo unit, and on this scale, thank God, it bottomed out at 50-pounds. Okay, that was good, but I badly needed real confirmation.

We made a few more drifts, but soon I was ready to get back to the dock to get an official weight. It was now after 6:00 P.M. and I knew my marina, Gone Fishing, would be closed for the night.

Fortunately, I remembered that Paulie's Bait and Tackle was having a Surf Fishing Tournament and would be open for the duration of the contest.

The best photo out of forty taken. Don't quit your day job for photography Rick.

The cruise back to the dock and the ride by truck over to Paulie's was tormenting. Eventually, I dragged the fish out of the cooler and onto the hook of the scale, and the needle did its customary wobble, finally settling in at 54.1-pounds. The monkey on my back had officially been removed. Screw you monkey!

Rick, cousin Mike, and Tom with the "monkey on my back."

In hindsight, I would have loved to have released that great fish. However, she was pretty worn out by the time I got her in the boat, and I highly doubt a release would have been successful. I must confess, I also wanted my wife, and a few of my fishing buddies to see this wonderful fish.

A photo of me and the 54-pounder, with the Montauk Lighthouse in the background, graced the cover of *The Fisherman* magazine a couple of weeks later. That's only the second time in my angling life I've been on the cover. A framed copy of the magazine hangs proudly in my den close by to the mount of the trophy striped bass. Since then, I have spent some major money on a very good

Bob and Mike had to take one more photo back at the dock.

scale that goes up to 100-pounds. Now I'll know instantly how big a bass is when I land it. Someday, God willing, the scale might reach into the 60 or 70-pound range, and if so, I can't wait for the battle!

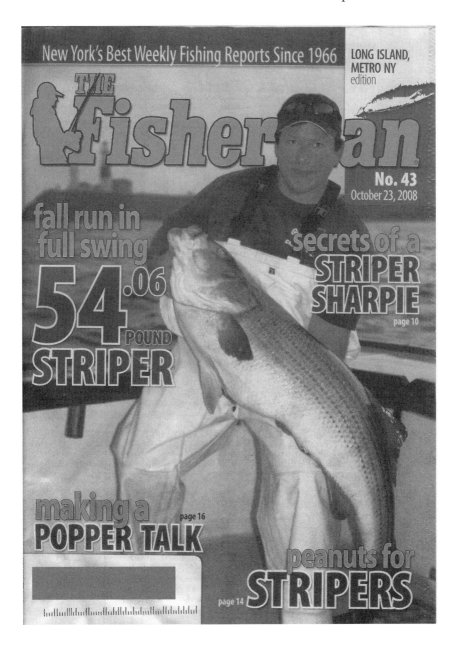

PART II

Chapter 7

Tools of the Trade

Big stripers have never been, nor will they ever be easy to catch. One can have the proper gear, hook the fish precisely, fight the fish flawlessly, and still a leader can part, a knot can fail, or a hook can simply pull free.

Personally, I'm fine with this prospect because striper fishing would get very boring, very quickly if every fish hooked was caught. Landing big stripers is special and I'm obsessed with repeating these encounters again and again. Conversely, losing big stripers blows, and I try to avoid these outcomes as much as possible. However, the big stripers I've lost haven't been in vain, and lessons learned have taught me it always pays to have the proper tools to get the job done.

Big stripers, like this 50-pounder caught by David Palmeri, require specialized gear to get the job done.

Rods:

Personally, I have used Lamiglas rods with great success while striper fishing for years. Over-the-counter Lamiglas rods that I highly recommend for striper fishing from a boat are the Tri-Flex series, and from lightest to heaviest the models I prefer are: BL 7025 (medium light), BL 7030 (medium), and BL 7040 (medium heavy).

The amount of quality choices available from other rod manufacturers such as Fin Nor, Penn, St. Croix, and Seeker is quite extensive. In my opinion, a basic striper rod, that will be used to target mostly school sized fish around 20-pounds, should have a line rating of at least 12 to 25-pounds. Targeting bigger stripers requires a heavier rod, and I'd recommend rods rated at 15 to 30-pounds for stripers above the 20-pound range. In areas that have deep water and strong currents, an even heavier rod rated at 20 to 40 or 30 to 50-pounds is a better choice.

A good way to judge the strength of any rod intended for striper fishing is to attach an 8-ounce sinker to the tip of the rod with a rubber band. Observe how much the tip flexes. If the tip bends too excessively the rod will probably lack the power to set the hook properly in a big striper's "tough" mouth.

I make most of the rods I use myself. Does this mean you should also be using custom rods? Honestly, a custom rod is crafted exactly to an individual's specifications. The more one fishes, the more exact these specifications become. The serial numbers of the Lamiglas blanks that I commonly use are: CGBT 841 ML, M, MH. The letters stand for Composite Graphite Boat Trolling; 84 represents eighty-four inches long; the 1 stands for one piece; ML- Medium Light, M-Medium, MH-Medium Heavy. These rod blanks are also very similar to the Tri-Flex over the counter rods described above.

In my opinion, to further refine the choices, the medium power blank/rod is the best choice when striper fishing with sinkers

A custom Grand Slam *rod made by me whipped this 39-pound striped bass.*

ranging from 8 to 12-ounces. This is a good description of the conditions I often encounter at Montauk. Striper fishing with heavier sinkers than 12-ounces, it's best to go with the medium-heavy power blank/rod. The only places where I come across such conditions are in the Race and Plum Gut off Long Island's North Fork. Drifting and casting in bays, inlets, or open water along the coast, the medium-light model is a good blank/rod choice. However, if a honker of a bass is hooked on this blank/rod, you'll probably be silently wishing for the power of the medium model.

Keep in mind, sometimes the specifications listed on rods by manufacturers can be misleading, and this makes buying through a catalog tough. Nothing beats holding a rod and feeling the flex and weight of the rod in your own hands. I suggest doing this whenever possible to avoid purchasing a rod that will not fit your needs.

Line guides are important, but their effects on angling are

often over looked. Quality guides are made with stainless steel or titanium frames with round inserts that are made of materials such as hardloy, alconite, or silicon carbide etc. These materials are all very hard, smooth surfaces that dissipate heat, and allow the main line to run freely through the guides. Avoid cheap metal guide inserts because they break and groove easily, and damaged or grooved guide inserts usually results in lots of broken lines and lost stripers. Always be sure to check rod guides, specifically the inserts, to insure that they are in good working order. Don't forget to also check the rod tip. Dropping a rod to the deck can easily cause the insert in the tip to dislodge, and this means trouble when fighting a large striper.

My trusty custom made Lamiglas CGBT-841 M rod whipped this 48-pound striped bass.

Reels:

I prefer conventional star drag reels in the 20 to 30-pound class for most striper fishing. Conventional reels offer more control and power than spinning reels do, and are also more easily manipulated

If stripers this size are the goal, don't go after them under gunned.

under the strain commonly generated by a big striper. If the intention is to do a lot of drifting and casting while striper fishing, I would avoid lever drag reels because the constant movement of the free spool lever on these types of reels often changes the drag setting. There are many good reels manufactured by Quantum, Penn, Garcia, and Daiwa that will all work well. Normally, the price of a quality striper reel starts at around $150 and goes up from there.

All Anglers have their favorite reels, and a couple of years ago I found a new favorite of my own. I had become extremely frustrated with the constant break down of my striper reels. So, I went into Paulie's Tackle in Montauk and proceeded to bitch about this problem. Paul reached into the counter and handed me a Fin-Nor OFC Offshore 20, and said, "Give it a try." I put the reel to work that night and ever since I have been slowly replacing my inventory of striper reels. The Fin-Nor OFC 20 reel is the smoothest functioning, most durable, reel I have ever used. In addition, it is also capable of imparting 35-pounds of drag pressure. This is an incredible amount of power to have in a relatively small package. In the future some other high-tech reel may win me over, but right now the Fin-Nor OFC Offshore 20 is tough to beat.

A Fin-Nor OFC 20 had no problem whooping this trophy linesider.

Let me discuss a reel's drag for a moment because this function of the reel is often misunderstood by some anglers. A reel's drag slows and tires a big fish when it runs and takes line off the reel spool. A drag functions like the anti-lock brakes on a car, and prevents the spool from locking up. A drag works best when it is neither too loose nor too tight. Too loose, a big bass will easily swim into structure, resulting in a lost fish. Too tight, and the spool will lock up and break the line, also resulting in a lost fish. In order to whip big stripers consistently it's crucial to always have a properly set reel drag.

Set the drag "tight and right" and more stripers this size will make it into the boat.

The normal standard used to set the reel drag is 1/3 the breaking strength of the main line. How is a reel drag set properly? A digital or spring scale is the answer. Attach the main line to the scale with a large snap swivel. Fasten the scale to a boat cleat and join the line to the scale. Pull back on the rod until the drag gives and check the scale to see where the drag gave way. Once the drag is set put on a heavy leather glove and pull line of the reel to develop a "feel" for proper drag pressure. In time, the scale won't be needed and muscle memory will do the trick.

I like to set my drag to 15-pounds when using 50-pound main line. I suggest testing your rod and reel combos with a scale to see how much drag pressure you can impart on your outfits. If the combos can't approach 15-pounds of drag, I'd suggest switching to heavier gear.

Main Line:

Make sure the main line is in good shape. Nicks and frays

are the enemy, so before each trip it's a good idea to strip off the last 10-ft of line, and re-rig. Monofilament is still good line and I use it often for diamond jigging, and bunker chunking. For these applications, I prefer 40-pound test Berkley Big Game or Hi-Seas Quattro. However, braided line is generally my preferred line of choice. I favor braid because it is more sensitive and thinner than equivalent sized monofilament. This thinner profile is beneficial because it allows the use of lighter sinkers. In addition, braided line has almost no stretch, and this makes hook setting more efficient. I now use Cortland Master Braid in 50-pound test for striper fishing, and it has yet to disappoint me.

If you hope to consistently catch stripers like this one, use lines strong enough for the task at hand.

I would be remiss if I did not mention a few drawbacks of braided line. First, nicked braided line is very tough to see, so keep your eyes peeled for this problem. Another hindrance is knot slippage, but this is easily overcome by either using a Palomar knot, or a 10-turn Improved Clinch knot. The final flaw of braided line is also one of its strengths: braided line has no stretch. Why is no stretch a flaw? Stretch in monofilament acts like a "spring" and absorbs much of the shock when a big striper shakes her head. With braid there is no "spring", and once a striper is hooked it's crucial to keep all slack out of the line, or the end result can be a thrown hook. Although, a new product called Zilla Braid by Spiderwire has a small amount of stretch in it that should help avoid thrown hooks. I can't stress enough that the inside of a striper's mouth is a tough medium for a hook to make solid purchase. In fact, many times I get a big striper into the boat, and the instant pressure on the line is eased, the hook simply falls out of the striper's mouth, and clinks to the deck.

Keep the rod tip high and use the flex of the rod to help keep the hook imbedded in the striper's mouth.

Gaffs and Nets:

I carry two gaffs and two nets for landing fish on my boat. If I'm going to keep a striper I use a gaff because gaffing is a more efficient way of ending the fight. I prefer a gaff that is at least 6-ft long, has a tapered end, and is armed with a hook that boasts a

3-inch throat. The length lets me reach out and "touch" a bass at quite a distance away from the boat. Over the years, I have observed many anglers wrongly try to put the gaff under the fish, and lift up to secure the fish. This usually results in a missed gaff shot. The proper way to gaff a striper is to point the gaff hook towards the water, reach over the fish's shoulder, and pull the gaff towards the boat to sink the hook.

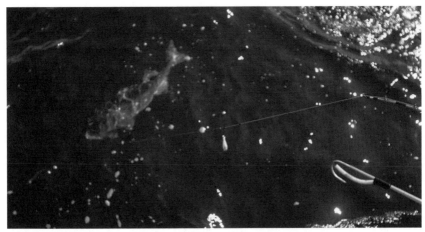

A gaff gives you more reach when intending to keep a large striper. It also ends the fight quicker. The quicker the fight, the less likely you'll lose the fish.

Nets seem easy to use, but I have witnessed some pretty comedic netting performances over the years. Be aware, nets with deep baskets are problematic on windy days because netting can easily tangle within the terminal gear at the worst of times. It's best to get into the habit of grasping the end of the net basket under your hands while holding the net. Once the fish is reachable, quickly release the net basket, and secure the fish.

I prefer nets that are at least 27-inches wide at the opening. However, a 50-pound striper has a girth of about 30-inches, so a wider net may come in handy at times. Always net the striper head first. Chasing the striper by the tail is a waste of time. When using a leader of 5-ft or longer, it's best to grasp the leader with a free hand in order to lead the striper into the net head first.

Left: Capt. Wayne Hermann nets a nice one for a charter. Big bass require nets with wide hoops and deep baskets.

Below: Always net the fish head first. Chasing them around by the tail is a waste of time.

Fish Handling-Fillet Gloves:

Fish handling and fillet gloves are great items to have onboard. Putting hands into a striper's raspy mouth for unhooking can result in scrapes and cuts to fingers. This may not be an issue when you catch a few stripers on a weekend, but after a few days where 15 to 20-stripers a trip are caught your hands are going to

Two kinds of fillet gloves, a Dexter #1377 soft stainless knife, a sharpening stick, a 12-inch cimeter, and a serrated Sani-safe knife are all good tools for cleaning stripers.

take a beating. Handling/fillet gloves will help protect your hands from these scrapes, and also from knife points and sharp dorsal fins. I prefer the gray metal gloves, but the tan Kevlar gloves will also do the job. However, knife points and striper dorsal fins can squeeze in through the mesh more easily with the Kevlar gloves. Over the years these gloves have saved me from many injuries, and I try never to clean or handle fish without them.

Pliers:

A durable pair of pliers with sharp cutting blades is essential to any successful fishing trip. A lot of money can be spent on wonderful pliers made of tungsten or some other alloy, but you can also lose a lot of money when that same pair of pliers is dropped overboard. Hey…it happens. Reasonably priced aluminum pliers

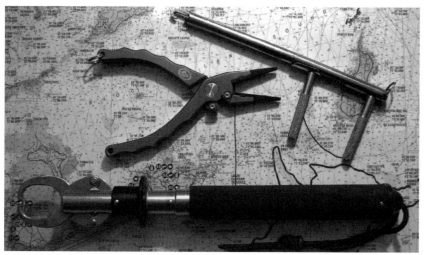

Pliers, de-hooker,and a gripper are standard equipment aboard the Grand Slam.

have recently hit the market. These pliers are very light, tough, and have cutting blades that can cheaply be replaced. Sharp cutting blades are crucial to cut thinner diameter braided line. These pliers seem to be manufactured by the same company, and have different names printed on them by distributors. I purchased several of these pliers for a reasonable price from Bass Pro's-Offshore Angler site, you can investigate them by searching "Aluminum Pliers". For the price they can't be beat, and if I manage to hold onto them for a few seasons great, if I lose them, no big deal.

Grippers and Lippers:

Grippers and lippers are handy alternatives to nets and gaffs. Some grippers also have scales built into them for conveniently weighing fish. I believe the Boga Grip is the best of the lot. However, the small numbers on this scale can be difficult for older eyes to read.

Grippers also come in handy for taking pictures of someone holding a fish when that certain "someone" is a bit squeamish about touching fish.

A Boga Grip helps hold this 42-pound striper while reviving her for a release.

De-Hookers

A good de-hooking device is a must to have onboard for deeply hooked stripers. Simply grab the hook at the bend, squeeze the grips together, and presto the hook is free. My favorite model is made of stainless steel and has performed flawlessly for me for 10-years and counting. I prefer the 8-½-inch models, and again the Bass Pro-Offshore Angler site has them as "Fish Hook Extractors" for less than $30.

This stainless steel de-hooker has served me flawlessly for over 10-years.

Fillet Knives and Sharpening Tools:

Cleaning the catch is much easier when done with proper knives. The Dexter fillet knife model #1377 is a 7-inch blade good for many types of fish. However, this knife is made of soft stainless, and it will rust if not used daily, or cared for at the end of the trip. For casual use, a hard stainless steel knife like the Dexter/Russell Sani-Safe Heading Knife model #114F 7-½-inch model is a better choice. I actually use 3-knives when filleting striped bass. I use the Dexter/Russell Tiger Edge serrated knife for the first cut through the skin and down to the bone. I switch to the Dexter #1377 or Sani-Safe #114F knife to remove the fillet from the bone. To remove the skin from a large fillet, I prefer a Forschner 10 or 12-inch cimeter knife. My knives are kept sharp with a sharpening stone or stick. I always touch the knives up before each use, and I'm not shy about re-sharpening while cleaning the catch. Keep the sharpening devices clean and dry for best results.

Gearing up properly with tools for big stripers will reward you in the long run. I understand every angler has an opinion on what works best for them. That's fine because I've just outlined what works best for me. I think it's wise to consider some of my recommendations. Keep in mind, substandard gear and tackle will normally work when fishing for smaller fish such as fluke or sea bass. However, use inferior tools on big stripers, and you'll regret it every time.

Chapter 8

Knots, Terminal Tackle, and Rigs

KNOTS

Good knots are essential for success in striper fishing. One could have huge bass biting their heads off right under the boat, but if the knots are tied poorly problems landing them will quickly arise. Practice tying knots often until they are perfect every time. If there is any doubt about the integrity of a knot, cut it and re-tie. Keep knots simple, and consistent. Once this is accomplished catching big stripers will become an easier endeavor.

John Fink with a 44-pounder caught with properly tied knots and rigging.

Always moisten the knot and main line before cinching up the knot. If this step is skipped the friction created during the cinch can cause the line to "burn" or weaken. Once the knot is complete, always trim off the tag end closely. Any excessively long tags, especially with monofilament leaders, can cause the knot to tangle with braid main braid line or other rigging.

Whenever a fish is lost, take a minute to figure out what went wrong. Crank in the line and inspect it for nicks or frays. If the hook or lure is gone, and all that remains is a "pig tail" on the end of the line, the knot failed.

Surgeon's Loop:

Let's start off with the easiest of all knots to tie-the Surgeon's Loop. This knot can be tied quickly, and for striper fishing it is mainly used to create a fixed loop for attaching sinkers or lures. To tie the Surgeon's Loop, form a loop at the end of the main line and tie in a loose overhand knot with this loop, and repeat with another overhand knot. In essence, a simple double overhand knot is being created. Lubricate the loop and pull tight slowly to form the knot. Trim off the tag end.

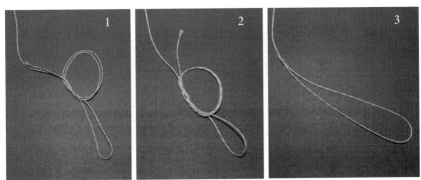

Step-by-Step demo of the Surgeon's Loop...

Palomar Knot:

Next up is the Palomar Knot. This knot is trusted by many

anglers to attach braided line to the eye of a hook, lure, or swivel. To tie the Palomar Knot, form a large loop with the end of the main line and pinch the end of the loop between the thumb and forefinger, so it can pass through the eye of the hook, lure, or swivel. Once through the "eye," form an overhand knot, and keep this knot loose in order for the hook, lure, or swivel to pass through this loop. Lube the loop with saliva and evenly pull on the double end of the main line, taking care to insure the knot cinches up tightly on the top of the "eye". Once the knot is tight, trim the tag end.

Step-by-Step demo of the Palomar Knot:

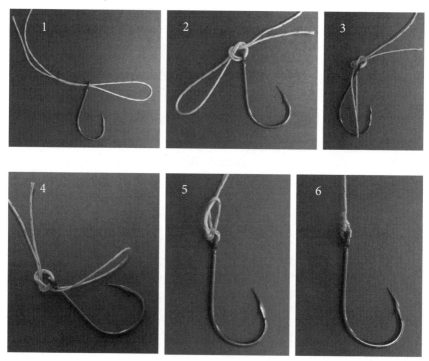

Modified Albright:

The Modified Albright knot will be used infrequently, so it is important to practice tying this knot in order to remember how to do it. The original Albright Knot was used extensively for attaching wire trolling line to a Dacron or mono backing. However, in my opinion the original Albright knot is inferior when joining braided line to a thicker monofilament top shot.

To tie the Modified Albright, form a large loop with the heavier line and pass about 10-inches of the thinner line through the loop of the heavier line and neatly wrap it up, and around the thicker loop 7 to 10-times. Reverse the thinner line and wrap it down around itself and thicker loop another 7 to 10-times. It is best to make the number of turns up and down the loop equal. Pass the thinner line back through the original loop in the same direction the knot was started. Lubricate with saliva and evenly pull tight on both ends of the thinner line, so the wraps up and down coil neatly next to each other. Don't be afraid to push the lines together to insure the coils form uniformly. Once the knot is evenly snugged up, trim the two tag ends.

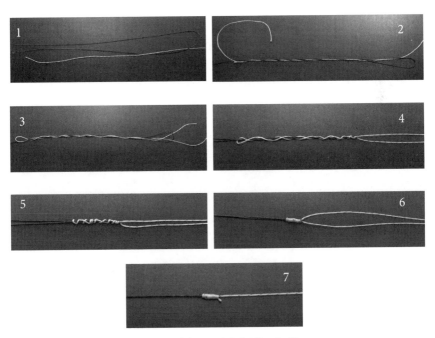

Step-by-Step demo of the Modified Albright Knot

The Improved Clinch Knot:

The next knot is "old faithful" for me. This knot is great for securing the main line or leader to a hook, lure, or swivel. There are some anglers who think this knot is inferior when used with braided line, and it is if the knot is tied wrong, but aren't all knots bad if tied wrong? The Improved Clinch Knot when tied correctly will hold to 95% the strength of the line it is tied on. I did my own testing with this knot and the result was the main line usually broke up ahead of the knot, which indicates the knot held stronger than the line itself.

To tie the Improved Clinch Knot pass the terminal end of the main line through the eye of the hook, lure, or swivel and wrap this line up around the standing end of the main line 10-times (if using monofilament line 4 to 6-times will do). Pass the terminal end back through the loop that has formed just above the eye of the hook, lure, or swivel. Be sure to come back with the terminal end of the main line and pass it through the other larger loop that has just formed on the standing main line. Lubricate the line and pull slowly on the main line to insure the coils snug up uniformly. Closely trim the tag end.

Step-by-Step demo of the Improved Clinch Knot:

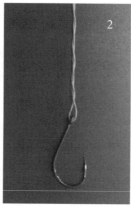
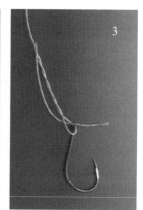

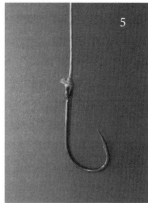

TERMINAL TACKLE

Hooks:

The hook is the most critical part of the terminal tackle. With that in mind, it is best to change hooks often when targeting big stripers. After many fish fights, or after becoming snagged in the bottom a few times, a hook will lose strength and can fail at the worst of times.

Modern hooks come out of the package incredibly sharp. However, this was not always the case. Many years ago I was fortunate to take a trip to Cabo San Lucas to fish for marlin. We trolled surface lures, and when a marlin was eyed in the trolling spread the captain would go into neutral, while the mate dropped back a live mackerel bridled to the hook. Several marlin were hooked, but each time we quickly lost the fish. After the fourth missed marlin I went to the cockpit and inspected the hooks. I discovered very dull hooks. Now, I speak no Spanish, and the mate did not speak any English. However, I held the hook up and shook my head in displeasure several times. Instantly, a large sharpening stone appeared, and the mate sharpened every hook on the boat. The troll resumed, and the next bite was a success, and after a great fight we released a 300-pound marlin. Lesson learned. I pay close attention to my hook points.

Circle hooks work great if the hook is left to do the work by simply allowing the striper to swim away with the bait, before setting the hook. I feel circle hooks are a better choice for inexperienced anglers who might have a problem detecting a bite. I prefer Gamakatsu Octopus Circles in size 8/0.

Circle hooks result in jaw or mouth hook-ups 90% of the time.

For the angler who has no patience when feeling a bite, J-hooks are a better choice. I prefer 8/0 Mustad Big Gun hooks or 7/0 Gamakatsu Octopus Beak hooks in the J-style. I don't snell the hooks to the leaders because I feel this is an inferior knot. I use either a Palomar or Improved clinch knot for the hook to leader connection.

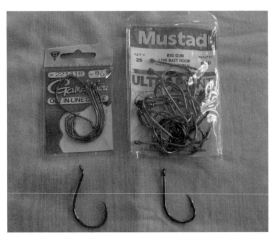

Circle hooks on the left, J-hooks on the right. Each season I find myself using more and more circle hooks.

Leader Material:

I prefer bulk 2-pound spools of monofilament for leader material. Line comes off these larger spools much straighter than it does off of a ½-pound spool, or small coil wheel. If smaller spools are favored, be sure to take the leader and stretch it out before using. This straightens the line and makes the leader line run truer through the water, and allows the bait to appear more natural.

Bigger spools result in nice straight leaders.

I use 40 to 80-pound monofilament leader for most of my striper fishing. Leader lengths and weights will change slightly according to the technique I'm using. These changes will be discussed within each of the coming chapters about techniques.

What about fluorocarbon leader? Fluorocarbon is touted to be invisible under water. However, water clarity in the Northeast is never crystal clear, so I don't think this feature is needed. If I did most of my fishing in the gin clear waters found in the Florida Keys I'd use fluorocarbon faithfully, but here I don't believe fluorocarbon is a necessity.

Snaps and Swivels:

Swivels and snaps are used to avoid line twists, and to aid in easy lure changing. I prefer Roscoe barrel swivels for jigging and fish finder rigs. Sizes I'm partial to are 3, 5, and 7, and range from 75 to 100-pound ratings. Many anglers prefer smaller swivels, fearing that a bass will see and shy away from larger ones. Again, water clarity is not usually an issue in striper fishing, and a striper doesn't have the brain capacity to really comprehend what a barrel or snap swivel is.

Snap swivels are convenient for changing lure sizes, or colors. I carry sizes between 5 and 2/0. I match the swivel to the size of the lure. Some snaps can be forced open by the power a large striper can impose during a fight. This problem can be eliminated by using *Tactical Angler Snaps*. These snaps will never open prematurely.

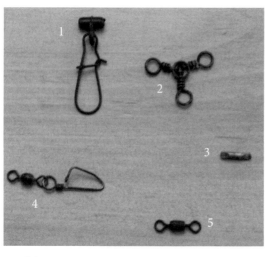

1- *Fish finder slide.*

2- *Three-way swivel.*

3- *Spro H-duty barrel swivel*

4- *Snap and barrel Swivel*

5- *Roscoe barel swivel*

RIGS

Fish Finder and Three-Way Rigs:

My bait rigs for striper fishing are normally either a fish finder or three-way rig. For the three-way rigs I prefer larger 3/0 and 5/0 size swivels because they do a better job at keeping the rigs from tangling.

To construct a fish finder rig start off by placing the plastic slide of the rig on the main line and tie on a 90-pound black barrel swivel with an improved clinch knot. To the other end of the barrel swivel attach the leader and hook. To finish off the rig, tie on the hook of choice and put an appropriate sized sinker on the snap that is attached to the plastic fish finder slide.

The three-way rig starts with a large 3/0 or 5/0 swivel. To one eye of the swivel attach the main line. To another eye attach approximately 20-inches of 40 to 60-pound mono leader. This line is the sinker tether. On this tether line, tie a surgeon's loop that is large enough to loop around a sinker ranging between 8 and 14-ounces. To the final eye of the three-way swivel attach the leader material with the preferred hook. I do all attachments with Improved Clinch Knots.

Casting and Jigging Rig:

For casting and jigging lures I prefer rigging with a short 18 to 24-inch monofilament shock leader of 40 to 60-pound test. I know many anglers like to attach this shock leader to the main line with a connection knot like the Modified Albright. However, I prefer a small black barrel swivel between the main line and leader. The barrel swivel helps negate line twist from the lure, and also acts as a nice gripping point to swing a school sized bass into the boat. On the end of the shock leader I attach a snap swivel for easy lure changing.

There we have it. Whenever I mention a knot or rig in any of the following chapters simply reference this chapter for precise instructions on how to complete the rigging.

Chapter 9

Drifting Eels - Montauk Style

I'm fortunate to catch many big striped bass each season. However, I'm a practical person and I realize the chief reason for my success is because I do most of my fishing at Montauk, NY. These famed East End waters of Long Island are often the place to be for catching big striped bass.

Steve Phillips with a chunky 38-pound striper caught on an eel drifted over Jones Reef at Montauk.

The Montauk concentration of stripers is easy to explain. The sea floor of Montauk abounds with structures including rocky reefs, boulder patches, and sandy shoals. All these bottoms attract and concentrate many forms of bait that striped bass feed on. Montauk is also home to swift currents. This harmonious environment of structure, bait, and current all merge to form an ideal habitat for striped bass. In fact, there are times when the sheer number of large stripers located off Montauk can cause any veteran striper angler to shake their head in wonder.

Top: *There are times in the season when it seems like every striper within the population is swimming off the Montauk Lighthouse.*

Below: *My Lowrance structure scan clearly shows small rocks on the sea floor and stripers (white specks) swarming above them.*

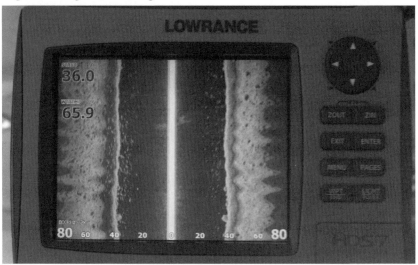

I value the challenge of catching striped bass of all sizes. But, I can't deny that catching big stripers is infectious. If big stripers are also your passion, you owe it to yourself to visit the waters of Montauk often.

Glenn Carr with an impressive October moon striper. Photo: Capt. Pete Mikoleski

In my opinion, the prime times are during the moon periods that occur between June and October. On the "moons," increased gravitational pull from the moon forces ocean currents to run swifter because tidal ranges are greater. These stronger currents are the best times for big bass to feed easily and aggressively.

A moon over Montauk always gets my adrenaline flowing.

Although there are many fishing techniques that are proven striper producers, in my opinion, the most enjoyable and challenging is drifting live eels. Eel baits will catch striped bass on both daylight and nighttime tides, and anyone who says differently doesn't know what they are talking about. If you want to view some video proof of dynamite daytime action on live eels, go to YouTube.com and search Thomas Mikoleski - "Montauk Stripers Grand Slam Charters 3 Days after Irene."

That being said, night tides do have their advantages. First off, striped bass are less skittish at night, so it's often easier to find yourself in the middle of a prolonged bite. Also on night tides (except for Fridays and Saturdays), there is usually less boat traffic on the water to interfere with where and how to fish for stripers.

Moon beams shining on the water along with a moving current usually result in nice Montauk stripers like this one. Photo Capt. Pete Mikoleski.

Some anglers feel that anyone can catch a striped bass on a live eel, and to some extent this may be true because there are times when stripers attack a live eel with a kamikaze like determination. However, this is an exception rather than a rule, and many times stripers, especially the big ones, are much more fickle in their attack. Keep in mind, between the moons when the currents run slower, catching striped bass on live eels can be a grind. On slower tides more big stripers will be caught by trolling large tubes or parachute jigs on wire line. But, if fishing live eels is a must for you even on "soft tides," try power-drifting to give the eel more life. In addition, lighten up on the leader and sinker weight, and also increase the length of the leader to as much as 15-ft.

Rigging Up:

I normally use a fish finder rig when drifting live eels. I prefer this rig primarily because it presents the bait naturally and usually keeps the rig from tangling. My go to leader for live eel fishing is a 5 to 6-ft length of 60-pound monofilament leader. Why do I like this length best? When eeling, there is always a chance of hooking a real whopper of a bass, and a 50-pound striped bass will be approximately 50-inches long. I usually like to keep my leaders longer than the length of the stripers I hope to catch. This is done so my abrasive resistant monofilament leader rubs against the striper's scales as opposed to my less abrasive resistant braided main line.

Me with a nice striper that was released. The gills are visible, but I assure you I am not touching them with my fingers.

Baiting Up:

In my opinion, big eels catch big bass, and I'd suggest using eels 15-inches and larger when specifically hunting for cow stripers. However, if getting bites from all sizes of stripers is the priority, smaller 8 to 12-inch eels should be used.

Getting a live eel on to the hook can be challenging when done incorrectly. The first thing needed is a "clean dry rag." Grab the eel by the head with the dry rag and smack the eel's **tail** sharply against the transom a few times. This will decrease the eels urge to swim. If whacking the eel is not done, there is a good chance that the squirming eel will wind itself up into the leader and create an "eel ball." Eel balls are slimy messes that usually results in the rig having to be re-tied. I never fish live eels without first whacking their tails. Some anglers may disagree and feel that placing live eels on ice is sufficient to "slow" them down. I agree, I also use ice, but I still whack them. I'm not a sadist, but even when iced down I've had too many eels ball up after warming up in sea water.

You might be thinking; *what is the big deal about one freaking eel ball?* Well, let me describe a scenario I've witnessed in the past. Let's assume you and a friend are fishing with me on the *Grand Slam.* We have been drifting for a while and the fishing is pretty slow. But then, suddenly, your buddy "Ralph" sets the hook into a good fish. I hear the reel drag protesting, so I call for the lines to be reeled in to avoid a tangle. In a few minutes Ralph manages to boat a 40-pounder, and its high-fives all around...awesome!

You are especially excited about Ralph's bass and dearly want one of your own. So, on the next drift you decide it's time for a fresh eel, but in the excitement of the moment, you did not whack the eel before placing it on the hook. I stop the boat for the next drift, and you grab the rod to drop the eel in the water. But now you discover that your eel is all balled up in the leader. The last thing you want, while Ralph is bragging about his 40-pounder, is an eel ball. Even if I grab another baited rod and hand it to you, there is little chance you will get that eel down in time to cash in on *this* drift. No big deal right? Abruptly, Ralph rears back on the rod, sets the hook and shouts, "Fish on!!" Just like that Ralph is into another cow. This fight is a repeat of the previous one, and in a few minutes an even bigger 45-pounder is now in the cockpit. Ralph is now strutting around like a proud peacock because he's such a great cow hunter, and you're standing there with a freaking eel ball...nice!

On the next drift you're re-rigged with a whacked eel and drop down to wait for a bite...and wait...and wait. But the next bite never comes. Guess what? It happens. And if you missed out of a

Angel Leon with a cow that was clearly hooked in the lip.

shot at a big bass because of an eel ball. Well, that really sucks, and that's why I avoid eel balls.

Hooking Options:

I hook the eel by placing the hook point through the bottom of the jaw and out an eye socket. This method works fine for me, but some other very good striper anglers prefer to hook their eels in various ways including through the bottom jaw and out the top of the head. Sideways through both eyes or sideways through the neck collar about an inch behind the eyes is also common. Bottom line, all hooking methods work, but if bites are tough to come by, try switching the hooking spot on the eel to see if a different method can coax a bite. One additional hooking technique to keep in mind, is putting two live eels on one hook. This presents a lot of "meat" for a stalking bass to sniff out, and sometimes this modification will produce a bite when all else fails.

The Proper Technique:

Always use a sinker heavy enough to keep the line angle to

the strike zone as straight up and down as possible when drifting. Six to 8-ounce sinkers will do the job at the beginning of the tide, but as the current picks up be sure to increase the sinker weight accordingly. Conversely, as the current slows down, decrease the sinker weight.

Walking the eel up, over, and back down any bottom contour changes is a crucial skill to master in order to catch big stripers consistently. I walk the eel by free spooling the rig to the bottom, and once the sinker hits bottom, I immediately lock up the reel, take 3-cranks on the reel handle, and bring the rod tip to a 45-degree angle. During the drift when the sinker touches bottom, I take 3-cranks on the reel handle, and re-position the rod tip at the 45-degree angle. I'm also in the habit of feeling for the bottom every minute or so, and repositioning my eel to the same 45-degree angle. This keeps my eel continuously in the striper's preferred feeding zone located 5 to 10-ft off the bottom.

Kevin Williams drove all the way from Pennsylvania to Montauk to catch this 49-pound striper on the Grand Slam.

During the drift a bite can come at any time, so pay close attention to the bait. No eating sandwiches, sipping adult beverages, or stargazing. Stay focused and be ready to react. When a bite comes, don't turn to a buddy and say, "Whoa, I think I just got a bite". If you do, the bite has just been blown. Keep in mind, on some trips you'll get 20-bites and hook most of them, on other trips you'll get 2-bites and miss them both.

Regardless the size of the striper taking the eel, the bite will feel like two sharp taps or tugs. At the instant of the bite it is imperative to drop the rod tip towards the water. This is called "bowing to the cow." The rod drop creates slack in the line, and gives the striper a chance to swallow the eel, and with it, the hook. "No bow, very often, no cow." After the bow, wait for the main line to come tight, and when it does it's time to set the hook. A J-hook necessitates a hard lift with the rod to drive the hook home. A circle hook requires "waiting for the weight," this allows the hook to slide out of the striper's throat and snag in the corner of the jaw. When it feels like the "weight" is about to pull the rod from your hands, smartly reel the handle a few times until the rod loads up with the weight of striper on the other end. At this point, if it will make you feel better to sock the hook home with a sharp lift of the rod, do so, but it's not necessary.

Rick Vidal hoists a 48-pound striper he whipped at a spot called Great Eastern.

Eel Scratches:

Slow fishing requires paying close attention to the little things. Check the eels often for very fine scratches on the eel's skin. Scratches mean the bites are happening, but they are not being detected. Concentrate a bit more on the task at hand because the stripers are taking the eels, but are spitting them out before the bites are detected.

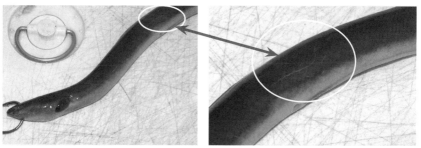

Eel scratches will tell you that your getting bites, but the stripers are biting very tentative tonight.

Don't Drag the Rig:

I find that many anglers like to drag the eel and sinker along the bottom. I can watch an angler's rod tip from 10-ft away, and tell if they are doing this. Simply put, if you drag, you will snag, and each snag costs about $5. Keep in mind, some angler's feel that the sound of the sinker bouncing against the bottom structure is a major turn off to big stripers. Truth be told, an occasional striper will be caught while dragging the eel along the bottom. However, many more stripers will be caught by keeping the eel in the "magic zone" just off the bottom.

Dead Eels:

Dead eels catch bass. I save the eels that have been on the hooks at the end of a trip and freeze them. On a future trip, I'll take the eels out of the freezer and let them thaw completely. Once thawed, rigor mortis will be gone and the eels will wiggly nicely when drifted behind the boat. In fact, the biggest bass I have ever caught was taken on a 16-inch, 4-month old, thawed out eel.

Once an eel has caught a striper, even if it's dead, do not stop using that eel until it's too ragged to be hooked properly. I don't know why, but when an eel has caught one striper, there is a good chance it will catch the next striper.

Captain Steve Kull seems pleased with his 30-pound striper caught on a "ripe" dead eel.

Right to the Light:

Montauk is home to many famous spots that produce big bass consistently. The list includes: the Elbow, Porgy Hump, Pollock Rip, North Rip, Midway Rip, and Great Eastern. In general, at the beginning of a current flow, start the drifts closer to the lighthouse. As current strength builds, move to other spots that are located north and east of the Point. The key to fishing any spot properly is to pull well up-tide of the structure and position the boat so the drift will put the eel right in front of a striper's lair.

Kenny Leon bested this symmetrical 42-pound striper on a dark new moon June night at a spot called the Elbow.

Rips:

During a strong current rips will form on the surface of the water. Rips are normally most visible above the highest points of the structure. Striped bass like to stage on the down-tide side of these high spots in order to stay out of the current flow. Rip lines are like a neon sign that shouts, "Striped Bass Here," and as long as the water near the rip is not in froth due to weather conditions, by all means do fish "here."

The Lazy Bones *works Pollok Rip, which seems to be on the verge of getting pretty bumpy.*

Use Your Electronics:

In order to place the baits in the prime zones it's key to rely on the boat's electronics. A chart plotter will put the boat right on the spot, and will allow the tracking of the drift. I recommend an angler save the spot/waypoint on the machine after a bite or hook up. Be sure to work that "mark" thoroughly before moving on. I always try to watch the fish-finder as I drift. If the spot is barren of marks or if I don't get a strike in a few drifts, I'll move on.

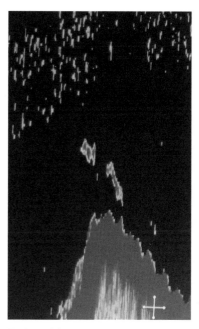

A lost eel on a drift could have been a striper stealing the bait, so make another drift just too be safe. However, a spot that doesn't produce means moving on. I may come back to it later in the tide, but I will not beat a dead horse just because I caught fish there in the past. The opposite also holds true. I will rarely leave fish to find fish in hopes of finding more or bigger ones.

This fish-finder photo clearly reveals 2-stripers feeding on the peak of a hill. The "lighter" squiggly lines up high is a school of bait.

Prime Time:

In my opinion, prime time to drift eels on any given tide is the 3 to 4-hours of peak current movement for that spot. This preference might be different in the areas you fish. At Montauk I'll take the stronger portions of the tide over the slower ones every time. A drift of 1.5-knots is usually the speed that will start to produce some bites. If the drift is slower than this I'd consider moving on to another spot where the current is running stronger. Take into consideration, if a big bass has been caught from a spot don't be in such a hurry to move in order to find the "next tide." In my experience, the biggest striper of the trip will often be hooked during the last hour of productive current stage.

Shallower Water:

There are times, especially on new moon nights, when big bass move into shallow water to feed on the beginning of the tide. I prefer to present my eel without any weight in such instances. To do this, I take the sinker off the snap of the fish finder rig and slowly

The Miss Mac *boats a nice striper.*

pull the main line off the reel. This allows the eel to drift "naturally" away from the boat. I said slowly, and I mean it. Pulling line off the reel too quickly results in a messy tangle. I count the pulls, and while deploying this technique, I have found that most bass bites will come at around 50-pulls off the reel. Once I'm satisfied with the location of my eel in the drift, I stop pulling line off the reel, and leave the reel in free spool, as I lightly feather the spool. Once a striper bite comes, I apply slightly more pressure to the spool to prevent an over-run, let the bass run for a count of five, lock up the reel, and set the hook.

The Fight:

The reel drag will whine loudly when a big striper is hooked. Hang on and enjoy the experience. Always keep the connection between you and the bass tight as possible. Stay smooth and avoid exaggerated pumping actions with the rod. Try to keep the rod tip high because this position keeps maximum pressure on the striper, but allows the rod to absorb much of the shock when a striper shakes its head during the fight.

Be prepared, when a big bass sees the boat she's going to run.

Once the striper gets close to the boat it's going to run again, so be prepared. If the bass is a big one, expect two or three of these boat side dashes. Remain calm. Soon the striper will be spent, and it will be time to land the bass by either netting or gaffing. Congratulations. All the hard work put into the pursuit of this great game fish has just paid off.

Kenny Leon hoists a chunky striper for another happy angler on the Grand Slam.

Never Forget the Eel:

In this chapter I have keyed in on drifting live eels Montauk Style. If an angler was to fish eels all season at Montauk, many striped bass would end up being caught by season end. However, eels are also reliable producers of striped bass along the entire coast. And if you are as obsessed with catching striped bass as I am, always remember that feeding stripers often find eels to be an irresistible temptation.

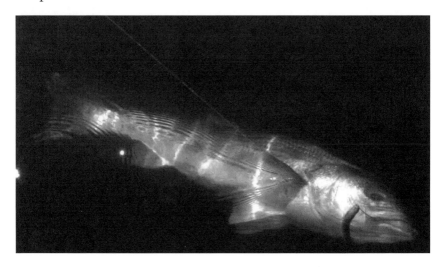

Chapter 10

Drifting the Bucktail

The fish catching ability of bucktail jigs is often underestimated by some anglers. However, bucktails do a fantastic job imitating a variety of prey species such as squid, spearing, and sand eels. Bucktails are lead heads with a hook, and hairs from a deer tail tied onto it. Some bucktails are tied with synthetic fibers. I would stay away from these types of bucktails because they are much less productive on stripers than those tied with deer hair. The reason being, deer tail hairs are hollow, and therefore a deer hair bucktail is more buoyant. In addition, deer hair pulses when the jig moves through the water. Buoyancy and pulsing both combine to give the bucktail jig the tempting action that stripers often find appealing.

Capt. Derek Grattan hoists a typical buck tailed striper caught on an evening flood tide at Montauk.

There are many styles of lead heads available and each has its own characteristics in the water. I prefer the "Smiling Bill" bucktails because the mouth is molded open. This shape catches water and causes the jig to glide through the water with an action that often triggers a striper to strike.

Color options are also varied. Keep in mind that most baitfish in the water will appear silver or white, so white is always the first color I use, but I also carry pink, yellow, chartreuse, black, and red. Chartreuse is a great color in deep water or on cloudy days. Red or black is often a good producer on dark new moon nights. Pink sometimes turns the trick when all other colors fail.

The Coyote *with a striper caught on a pink bucktail off Long Island's North Fork*

The next choice is whether to use fixed or swing hooks on the bucktails. Most bucktails come with fixed hooks, but by shopping around you can find swing hook bucktails such as the Uncle Josh brand. Swing hook bucktails have an advantage because the hook can easily be changed when they become rusted. Some anglers also feel that swing hook bucktails produce more action when retrieved or drifted. This subtle modification in action can sometimes make the difference in getting bites.

This chartreuse swing hook bucktail was appealing to this feeding striper.

Give Three-Waying a Try:

There are many ways to present a bucktail when striper fishing. The method I prefer most is three-way drifting. This method is used with great success off the East End of Long Island, in Plum Gut, and the Race. Nonetheless, I'm certain this method will also be effective anywhere along the coast where currents are strong enough to make the bucktail slide along through the water when drifted.

Grand Slam mate Kenny and Emily Sherman with a nice school sized striper caught to the south of the light.

There was a time when I had my doubts about using the three-way rig at Montauk. Well, I tried it anyway, and ever since I have caught a heck of a lot of Montauk stripers on it. So I'm confident that anywhere where a drift speed of at least 1.5-knots can be achieved, three-waying the bucktail will produce stripers.

A yellow bucktail drifted close to Block Island fooled this striper for Eric.

The Three-Way Rig:

The construction of the basic three-way is described in chapter 8, but here are a few additional points to keep in mind when using the rig with a bucktail. Sinker weights will range from 6 to 20-ounces depending on current strength. Sinkers are expensive, but they are cheaper than bucktails. As a result, many anglers like to tie a half hitch knot into the sinker line at the half-way point. This way, if the sinker becomes snagged in the bottom the half hitch will break the sinker line, allowing the bucktail to be saved. That being said, some anglers don't like to use the half hitch because they feel too many sinkers will be lost, and they prefer trying to muscle the whole rig out of the snag. The choice is yours.

The length of the leader to the bucktail is an important part of a productive rig and usually varies from 4 to 8-ft. The strength of the leader is also a key and usually ranges from 60 to 125-pound test. In areas like the Race, where deep water, strong currents, and lots of toothy bluefish are the norm, go with 8-ft of 80 to 100-pound leader. In Montauk, or other areas where the current rarely goes over 3-knots, stick with a 6-ft leader of 60-pound test. However, never go too light with leader size because the diameter of the leader line actually catches the current and gives the bucktail more "life".

This husky bass found it's way aboard the Rainbow *via a bucktail drifted in the Race,*

Most anglers use 1¼- ounce bucktails. Lighter bucktails can also be used to get more float, but on smaller bucktails it's tough to find large 6/0 and 8/0 hooks that are needed to stand up to the power of big striped bass. (Note: With swing hook bucktails any size hook can be placed on the bucktail.)

Bucktail Trailers:

I never use bucktails without some kind of attractant trailer. I prefer Uncle Josh Pork Rind in size 70-S. Others anglers commonly add scented Berkley Gulp Grub Tails, Shads, Pogys, or other soft bodied swimbaits. Some especially cunning anglers like to use fresh squid, fluke, bluefish, or striped bass belly strips on their bucktails. Truthfully, anything that adds a little wiggle or vibration to the bucktail will work.

Pork rind is my preferred choice because it's a tough product that lasts a long time on the hook. In my opinion, pork rind becomes even more effective after it gets softened up a bit by striking stripers and blues. My favorite pork rind colors are all white, red/white, yellow/white, and black. Rind colors can be mixed by doubling them up on the hook to match the color of the dominate bait the striper's are feeding on. I find that a red/white pork rind teamed up with a black pork rind is especially productive for me.

Yellow and red Uncle Josh pork rind teamed with a chartreuse bullet head bucktail is a consistent producer in Plum Gut.

Every baitfish in the striper's world has darker upper bodies and whitish bellies, so when attaching the two-color rind to the hook keep the darker color up and the lighter side down. I like to mix bucktails and rind colors with other anglers fishing with me in order to find out if there is a dominate color pattern on any given tide.

Montauk's North Rip is always visible when the current is moving, and is a reliable spot to find stripers

Where to Start:

I normally cruise over areas that have produced for me in the past and watch my fish-finder closely to see if I can spot bass or bait. I'll set up for a drift once marks are found. During daylight I'll also be on the lookout for working birds that reveal patches of bait fish. Remember, surface rip lines indicate bottom depth changes, and when no marks or birds can be found these areas are the prime places to drift a bucktail.

Coyote hooked up again just in front of a rip in the Race.

Proper Technique:

Successful three-way bucktailing is a lot harder than it appears. First off, always be sure the hook point is razor sharp, and after each drift re-check the point because bumping into bottom structure will quickly dull a hook. Make sure the reel drag is set properly because if the drag is set too loosely it's impossible to set the hook into the hard structure of a striper's mouth.

Drop the three-way rig to the bottom and the instant the sinker touches bottom lock up the reel, and take 3 to 5-turns on the reel handle. It is now best to keep the rod tip pointing towards the water. (Note: This is completely opposite from how I recommend fishing with live eels.) Try to keep the bucktail rig high enough off the bottom, so the bites can easily be differentiated from the sinker or rig touching the bottom. Dragging the bottom with the rig will cancel out the sensation of the bite, and eventually result in a snagged rig. If possible, watch the fish-finder throughout the drift, and raise or lower the rig as the bottom depth changes. If the fish-finder can't be viewed, it is best to drop down and touch the bottom, and quickly take 3-cranks on the reel every 30 to 60-seconds.

Capt. Phil Kess (pictured with a nice blackfish) doesn't like it when you try to pet the bass upon a bite. He recommends setting the hook with some gusto.

While drifting it's crucial to swing the rod tip **hard** to attempt a hook set whenever the slightest bite is felt. My good friend Capt. Phil Kess of the charter boat *Fishy Business* says, "You're not petting these fish, you're trying to hook them." This description is perfect. If there is no hook up on the rod swing, this probably means the sensation felt was the sinker touching bottom. Take three more cranks on the reel, and return the rod tip pointing towards the water. Continue walking the bucktail along the structure, and swinging at anything that feels like a bite. This is the proper drill for the entire trip .

This angler is locked in on an early May drift aboard the Nancy Ann IV *in Plum Gut.*

Pay Attention:

No matter the size of the striper, the hit on a bucktail can be unbelievably tentative, and this is especially true when the current stage is off its peak. Keep in mind, it is always better to attempt a hook set at what might be a bite, than to lag behind and thinking, gee…was that a bite? Reason being, the instant a striped bass gets a taste or feel of the bucktail jig the striper is going to know in an instant whether it is something it wants to swallow or something it wants no part of. The striper must be hooked before the bucktail is spit out, or the battle will be lost before it ever began.

His attentiveness paid off moments later with a scrappy schoolie.

Short Drifts:

Often, stripers will feed on very small bottom pieces that only rise slightly off the bottom. Short drifts are the keys to success in such scenarios. In addition, watching the fish-finder and chart plotter intently is also essential because if the boat is not positioned precisely, a small pod of feeding fish can easily be missed on a short drift.

Short, fast drifts can be a problem when there are other anglers fishing with you. All onboard must be conditioned to be ready the instant the boat is stopped in order to avoid tangles. A slow angler to the rail should be told to keep their line out of the water because by dropping down late in the drift, all that is usually accomplished is tangling with other anglers already in the water.

Use the Engine:

A slow drift speed caused by either wind against the tide, or a weak current does not bode well for three-waying. However, drift speed can be increased by power drifting with the engine(s). In addition, if on a moon tide and the drift is too fast, the engine can be bumped into gear to stem the tide, and slow the drift of the vessel. This is not an optimal fishing situation because stemming the tide usually causes the lines to drift in the current at an awkward angle. Nevertheless, it will accomplish presenting the bucktail at a more appealing speed to the stripers.

Joanna Sherman was red hot with a white bucktail on this beautiful September evening.

I also often power drift when birds are working over bait on an open flat bottom. Scenarios like this are common in the spring and fall months off our coastal beaches when bass and bait are migrating.

Diving birds are always a sure sign that bait and game fish are in the area.

This fish-finder photo reveals stripers feeding from 20 to 60-ft in the water column.

Upon finding working birds, I slowly move into the area of diving birds until stripers are marked solidly on the fish-finder. I hit save on the chart plotter, move up-current 100-yards or so, and turn the bow towards the spot where I marked fish. I get the bucktail over the side and bump the engine and pilot the wheel to maintain a proper drift speed and direction, so the bucktail drifts right into the feeding stripers. A power drift speed between 2.5 to

3.5-knots seems to work best for me. This speed increase will impart additional lift on the bucktail, and it will be necessary to use heavier sinkers. On a flat bottom, any taps felt are usually bass or bluefish bites, so swing often and hard when any taps are felt.

Three-waying the bucktail is a very exciting and productive method for catching striped bass of all sizes. Some time will be needed to learn the proper "feel" for this technique. However, once the "feel" is acquired an angler has taken some mighty big steps towards becoming a very good striped bass fisherman.

Tim Sherman is deadly with a white bucktail and black pork rind when drifting aboard the Grand Slam *in the Montauk Rips.*

Chapter 11

Trolling Wire Line

Trolling lures on wire line is a very efficient technique for catching striped bass of all sizes. In fact, trolling has probably put more stripers in the boat than all other angling methods combined. There are a few reasons why wire line trolling is so productive. First, it allows an angler to probe lots of water quickly in order to find concentrations of stripers. Second, when water current is running slow, trolling presents the lures with action that often triggers stripers to strike. Thirdly, wire line gets the lures deep into the water column with pin point accuracy, and this is where stripers do most of their feeding.

Gearing Up:

Wire line trolling requires different gear from other methods of striper fishing. The most durable reel for wire line trolling is the Penn 6/0, 114H. This durability comes at a cost because the reels are very heavy. The smaller Penn 4/0, 112H is lighter and will also do the job.

Wire line trolling rods need to be extra strong. If big spoons are going to be the primary lures trolled it is best to use longer 7-1/2 to 8-ft rods that have a "slower flexing" action throughout the blank. Seeker makes a rod specifically for bunker spoons. The model number is BA-1153-8-WL. Lamiglas also makes a blank BT 96 3M when cut at the top of the blank to accept a #12-tip is perfect for trolling big spoons. My rods built on these blanks have "slick" or aluminum butts. This is so the rod can more easily be removed from the rod holder when a big bass is bucking on the other end of the line.

Shorter, stout rods will do the job when trolling lures other than bunker spoons. However, be sure any rods chosen to troll wire line have guide inserts of silicon carbide, nitride, or some other material that will stand up to the abuse of wire line. Lamiglas makes a great over the counter rod that strives to put the "fun" back into wire line trolling. The model number is BL 5630, and is rated for 20 to 40-pounds. Team this rod up with a Penn 4/0, spooled with 40-pound wire, and the result is an outfit that is much lighter for an angler to handle, but still strong enough to whip some mighty big stripers.

My Lamiglas BT 96 3M blank has a slow flexing action that is prefect for bunker spoons.

Personally, I use 400-ft of 60-pound soft stainless steel wire, but 40 or 50-pound wire will also work. There is another wire option on the market called Monel that is softer and less prone to kinking, but it's more expensive than stainless wire.

Wire line has to be marked at intervals to know the depth the lures are swimming. I prefer to mark the wire with the following color sequence: Red 100-ft, Yellow 200-ft, and Green 300-ft., like a traffic signal. You can mark the wire yourself by winding on short lengths of colored plastic coated wire that are remnants left over from telephone linemen. This means stretching all the wire out somewhere and placing the marks. I've done this, and it is a pain in the butt. A better option is to make a homemade jig with a line counter and spool holder. I've gotten lazier over the years and found it's easier to simply have a local tackle shop spool up the reels and mark the wire.

The end of the wire line should be prepared for the leader by attaching #3, or #4 heavy duty *Spro* swivel with a Haywire twist, make sure the swivel is small enough to pass through the rod tip. To the other end of the barrel swivel attach 15 to 20-ft of 80-pound monofilament leader. To complete the rigging attach a large snap and barrel swivel.

Umbrella Rigs:

Most umbrella rigs come with short tubes dangling from wire arms on 6 to 10-inch monofilament leaders. Recently, rubber shads have become popular. However, I prefer the tubes because they stand up better to bluefish, while shads quickly become shredded. I also know anglers that have great success by switching the tubes on the umbrella rig for small bucktails or plugs.

I prefer darker hued tubes for stripers. Brighter colored tubes tend to attract more bluefish. I normally change out one of the short mono leaders to a longer 3 to 5-ft leader. This presentation gives the impression of an injured baitfish having trouble keeping up with the school. Usually, 80% of the hook ups will come on this straggler tube. Some big striped bass can also be caught by replacing the small center tube with a larger 12-inch surgical tube attached to a 3 to 5-ft leader.

Be careful when placing the umbrella rig in the water because the tubes can easily tangle. I stand on the port or starboard side of the cockpit and place the rig into the turbulence-free water slightly forward of the stern. I quickly free-spool the rig down a few feet, and once all the tubes are underwater, I'll allow the wire to be pulled off the spool, as I thumb the spool slightly. This will avoid most tangles.

A triple header of school sized stripers on an umbrella rig.

Double and triple headers of stripers commonly occur with umbrella rigs when bass are schooled up. In fact, many years ago, while trolling an umbrella rig off Long Island's South Shore, I hooked up with what I thought was the striper of my dreams. The hit came with 300-ft of wire in the water. A lot of wire was stripped off the drag after the strike, and it was some time before I was able to gain control of the situation. It was a long and exhausting fight. Eventually, I got the umbrella rig within 20-ft of the boat, and my emotions quickly sank when out of the depths appeared 3-striped bass, all in the 20-pound class, attached to my umbrella rig.

Spoons:

Large spoons, commonly called Bunker Spoons are great producers of bigger striped bass. This is especially true for anglers who fish the waters off the New York Bight and New Jersey Coast. Large spoons are excellent mimics of big baits such as bunker, shad, or herring. Tony Maja, Reliable, and Secret Spoon are all manufacturers that produce quality spoons.

Years ago, I was fortunate to meet Capt. Ronnie Lepper of the charter boat *Kim*. Ronnie was one of the best bunker spoon trollers of all time. His home waters were anywhere from Sandy Hook, NJ to Fire Island, NY. Ronnie used to say, "Use any color bunker spoon you want as long as that color is white". I agree, but it does not hurt to have chartreuse or dark green spoons aboard, too.

A white bunker spoon duped this 20-pound striper.

Sometimes, I place Mylar tape strips on the spoons in order to give the lures a little more flash in the water. It is also a good idea to add a large stainless steel split ring (rated at about 170-pounds) to the attachment hole on the head of the spoon. This alteration will allow the bunker spoon to have more "wobble" when trolled.

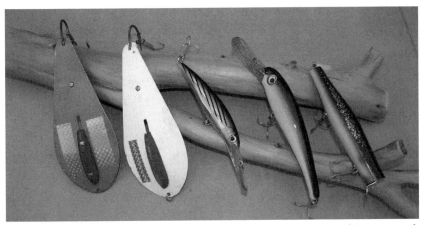

Green and white bunker spoons, Rapala deep diver, Mann Stretch 25, and Danny metal lip swimmers are all in my trolling arsenal.

The trick to trolling bunker spoons is moving at the proper speed so the spoon swims correctly: too fast and the spoon will catch only bluefish, too slow and the spoon will only catch the bottom. The spoons produce best when the rod tip is moving as follows: A thump, thump, followed by a prolonged deeper t-h-u-m-p, back to another thump, thump, and a prolonged deeper t-h-u-m-p, etc.

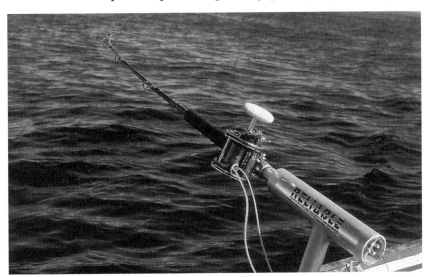

An out-rodder is a must when trolling bunker spoons.

With this rhythm, the spoon is wobbling from side to side and occasionally flipping over. If the rod tip is doing a constant: thump, thump, thump, thump...the spoon is just spinning in the water. Try watching the lure 20-ft from the stern (if possible keep the lure out of the prop wash), if the spoon is digging and dodging from side to side, excellent!

Spoons work best with an "out-rodder" that allows the lines to run a little deeper in the water. The out-rodder also gives the lines an extra few feet of spread between the port and starboard lures. This diminishes the likelihood of tangling the spoons in a turn.

Parachutes:

Another top producing lure is the parachute jig. This lure is nothing more than a long haired lead head similar to a bucktail, but instead of deer hair it is tied with long synthetic fiber hair. A properly jigged parachute simulates a squid. It takes a little talent to impart the right action, but once mastered, parachutes are prolific producers of striped bass.

A parachute jig and pork rind is a consistent producer with stripers of all sizes.

I prefer Andrus 2 to 4-ounce parachutes, in either chartreuse or white, but sometimes I'll sneak a pink one into the water. Two-ounce parachutes will have more action when jigged and 4-ounce parachutes will probe deeper in the water. I normally tip the lure with an Uncle Josh 70-S red and white pork rind, but sometimes white, or yellow rinds will make a difference.

Once the parachute lure is at the proper depth it is best to sweep the rod with short, quick pumps that cause the jig to dance and dart. Sounds easy, doesn't it? Yes, I think so to, but sometimes it's tough for an angler to get it just right.

Work the parachute correctly on wire line, and you can catch stripers like this until it feels like your arms are going to fall off.

Here's a more detailed description of the technique. Stand in the rear of the starboard cockpit and point the rod towards the water at a 45-degree angle with the right hand on the fore grip, and left hand holding the rod butt. Twist the rod so the reel is facing the water and pump the rod tip down to the water's surface nice and snappy, occasionally smacking the surface of the water with the wire. Allow the rod to come back to 45-degrees, wait for the wire to come tight, and pump again. The proper timing should be about one-pump every two seconds. Always be prepared for a strike because when it comes it is a startling jolt capable of pulling the rod right out of your hands. Keep in mind, while jigging the parachute, it is important to take in a few feet of line, or let out a few feet of wire line every minute or so. This is so the wire line won't fatigue at the rod tip. If this adjustment is not made the wire line will eventually break right at the rod tip.

Large Tubes:

Large single tube lures are very effective on striped bass. This is especially true in the month of August at Montauk and Block Island. Tube lures come in many assorted lengths, thicknesses, and colors. Generally, I like tubes that are at least 12-inches long, but I commonly use them as long as 36-inches. I have had the most success trolling Sekora and T-Man tubes, but many veteran charter boat captains make their own tubes, so they can fine tune the lures until just the right action is achieved. When working deepwater and heavy currents, I prefer bigger bodied tubes. In shallower water and

A Large red tube and two slices of Uncle Josh pork rind enticed this Block Island striper into biting.

slower currents, thinner bodied tubes get the nod. Black and red are my preferred colors, but if the water is cloudy go with brighter greens and yellows.

In New England these lures are always trolled with a piece of fresh sea worm as an added enticement. This set-up is commonly called a Tube and Worm rig. I have used tubes successfully with sea worms, but other enticers such as Berkley Gulp or Uncle Josh Pork Rind are more convenient and cheaper options.

Plugs:

I also troll metal lip plugs like Gibbs Danny Swimmers. Plugs aren't as popular with trollers as they once were, and I'm not sure why. However, these lures have accounted for a lot of big cows

Capt. Erik Weingartner used a white darter to troll up this striper that was feeding on a school of squid.

over the years. In fact, my brother and I caught our first big stripers aboard the Rainbow, with Capt. Bob Rocchetta, by trolling white and yellow Danny Swimmers in the rips off Block Island. Darters are also good plugs to troll, especially when squid are abundant.

Deep diving plugs are also popular, mostly because they can be trolled without wire line. My favorite deep divers are Mann's Stretch-30 and 25's. The Stretch 30 is supposed to run at a depth of 30-ft with 150-ft of 50-pound monofilament in the water. The Stretch 25 will give you 25-ft of depth with 150-ft of 30-pound monofilament.

A blue Mann Stretch 25 did the trick with this North Rip striper.

Keys for Successful Trolling:

Wire line needs to be dealt with differently than other types of line. First off, when letting wire out behind the boat, do so with the reel clicker on. This will slow the release of wire and help avoid overruns on the reel spool. Wearing a pair of work gloves while letting the wire out is a good idea because even properly trimmed wire can still cut your fingers. Avoid kinks in the wire at all costs. A kink weakens the line, and eventually causes the wire to break. So, be sure to always reel the wire back onto the spool nice and tight.

At a speed of 3-knots, wire line will sink approximately to 5-ft of depth for every 50-ft of wire released into the water. If more depth is needed, weighted drails can be added. Each 4-ounces of drail weight will add an additional 5-ft of depth. Do not attach the drail next to the lure because this will kill the action. Instead add the drail between the end of the wire line and before the monofilament leader. It is now necessary to hand-line in the final length of the leader into the boat. As mentioned several time already, striped bass usually seem to prefer the zone of water 5 to 10-ft off the bottom. So, when trolling it is a good idea to present the lures in this most productive area of the striper's realm.

Whenever there are two wire line rods in the water, it is crucial to turn v-e-r-y gradually. If the turn is too tight the lures will tangle and untangling two rods with 300-ft of wire in the water is a horror. Also, when making a turn, the lure on the inside rod will run deeper in the water column than the line on the outside rod. If you want a lure to run a little deeper at anytime make a gradual turn or drop the transmission into neutral for a few seconds.

Troll slowly to land big stripers like this 50-pound brute.

Proper trolling speed is crucial when after big bass. The most productive trolling speed is between 2 and 3.5-knots. Most outboards can troll in this range because they have relatively small props. On bigger inboard boats it can be difficult to troll slowly enough. Such vessels often have a trolling valve on the transmission that allows the shaft to slip, and turn the prop slower.

Wind and current will always affect the trolling speed. In strong current areas, such as Montauk, it is best to troll 90-degrees to the direction of current flow. Occasionally turn the bow directly into the current in order to sweep the lures into the most productive parts of the rips that lie on the edges of the eddies. Sometimes the bites will only come when trolling in one direction in relation to the current. To keep the bites constant, pull the lines in, and reposition the boat to troll in the direction that is producing best. Wind will also affect trolling speed. A strong wind on the stern will cause the boat to troll faster. Often, it pays to make a long run with the wind, turn around, and troll into the wind to slow the trolling speed.

A big green tube was the downfall of this 34-pound Block Island linesider.

Summary:

Trolling is a great method to use when searching for striped bass. I normally troll when the current is running slow or slacking, because this is when striped bass will be spread out. Trolling wire also allows an angler to catch big striped bass under adverse sea or weather conditions that often render other angling methods ineffective. In short, trolling is an important tool for a successful striper angler to have in their quiver.

Chapter 12

Live Lining and Bunker Chunking

Bunker is an oily nutritious baitfish that travel in large dense schools and are a major food source to many game fish, especially stripers. Finding a school of bunker can at times be frustrating. The search is simpler on flat calm days when bunker can be seen at a distance finning or flipping on the surface. A tight concentration of boats is also a good sign that bunker are in the area. Before attempting to snag bunker in close vicinity to other boats, take a minute to assess the situation. Move slowly and be courteous to those already on the bait.

Finning bunker are easier to find on calm days.

Snagging a Few:

A 7-ft medium to heavy action spinning combo spooled up with 20-pound braid or monofilament line is a good snagging outfit.

Attach a weighted snagging hook to the main line on the snagging outfit. Once within casting distance of a bunker school, launch the snagging hook into the pod, and let the hook sink for a couple of seconds before beginning a quick retrieve. When the hook is felt banging into bunker, make long sweeps with the rod to snag one. If all goes well it shouldn't be long before there are enough bunker in the live-well to start fishing.

Some anglers use a cast net to capture their bunker quickly and efficiently, and this is a great skill for any angler to master. Unfortunately, I'm not one who posses this skill…yet.

Bob Petersen used a frisky live lined bait to dupe this fine striper.

Live Lining catches Big Bass:

Baiting with a whole bunker is a great way to catch big striped bass. I prefer rigging with 4/0 VMC extra strong treble hooks on a 5-ft leader of 60-pound test leader when live lining bunker. I normally hook the live bunker one of two ways. The first way is to place one hook of the treble into the upper mouth and out one of the nostrils. Bunker hooked this way usually stay near the surface and often attract explosive top water strikes. The second way is to hook the bunker behind the dorsal fin near the meaty part of the tail. Bunker hooked this way will normally swim down and away from the boat. This method is beneficial to get the bunker down and away from a hungry school of bluefish.

The white patches in this pod of bunker are bluefish raiding the school.

Seven Seconds to Victory:

I like to place a fish finder rig on my main line, so sinkers can easily be removed or added. I usually fish with two rods that are each baited with a whole live bunker. One rod gets no weight, and the other gets a 1 to 3-ounce bank sinker to the fish finder. This helps me cover different depths.

Fish the whole bunker close to the school because the bunker on the hook is injured, and will be swimming erratically. This is enough to attract the attention of a feeding striper. I like to hold one rod and dead stick the other. Both reels should be in free spool with the clicker on. Once a pickup occurs grab the rod, release the clicker, lightly thumb the spool, and let the bass run off with the bunker for 7-seconds. This can be the longest 7-seconds of your life. After waiting, lock up the reel, take the slack out of the line, and set the hook with a powerful lift of the rod.

Bunker Baits equal big bass.

Stripers under a bunker school can sometimes be lazy and ignore live bunker baits. In order to coax a bite on such occasions, cut up a live bunker into chunks and cast out the chunk weighted down with a 5-ounce sinker. Keep the chunks close by the bunker school. This is also a good option when bluefish are raiding a bunker school and it's tough to get a live bunker past the bluefish. Always remember, less aggressive stripers often prefer to cruise below the bunker school and feast on the bunker scraps chopped up by bluefish.

I'd recommend giving a school of bunker 20-minutes to produce a striper. After that time it is usually best to search out another bunker school that might be more productive. It might be tough to leave a school of bait, but if there are no bass on the school, no bass can be caught.

Can't Get Live Bunker, Use Chunks:

If you don't have access to live bunker, the other option is to anchor up on some structure, and use store bought bunker to start a bunker chunk chum slick. Whenever possible I highly recommend using fresh bunker chunks. I know this is sometimes easier said than done, but the fresh stuff is often the key to success. However, if frozen bunker is all that's available, I'd skip it, and instead purchase frozen mackerel because this bait produces better striper action than the frozen bunker does.

Bunker chunking can produce fast action with stripers this size.

Simply put, big bass love **fresh** bunker chunks. On July 4, 2008, Capt. Phil Kess of the charter boat *Fishy Business*, decided to take advantage of very light holiday boat traffic, and anchored his vessel over some very rocky structure located off Long Island's North Fork. Capt. Phil proceeded to establish a chum slick with fresh bunker chunks to get the resident stripers into a positive feeding mode. The anglers on the charter were eager to start fishing and tossed chunks into the swirling current. The very first striper to take a chunk that afternoon was a 70-pound monster that was fought to the gaff by angler Mike Columbus. Soon, another huge bass of

54-pounds was also landed on a bunker chunk. When the fifty-four was laid next to the seventy, the size disparity was almost comical.

A bunker head drifted back into the slick at Great Eastern fooled this beautiful striper.

I like to cut bunker for chunking so I get four meaty pieces of bait from each bunker. The tail piece is useless because it does nothing but tangle the rig. The head chunk is the best bet for fooling a big striper. On a hard running current it is best to thread the hook point through the lips so the gap of the hook helps keep the mouth closed.

If the current is running slowly the hook can be placed in the collar of meat located just behind the gill plates. The two pieces

Top: Hook the head chunk this way when the tide is running hard.

Below: This is also a prime chunk because it contains the gut cavity.

of bunker that includes the organ cavity is the "fillet mignon" of the bunker. It is best to place as much of the guts onto the hook as possible. I like to place the guts and heart onto the hook first, and thread the hook through the meaty portion of the chunk.

Hook the gut cavity chunk this way when intending to cast it out away from the boat.

Avoid weaving the chunk onto the hook. Just hook it once and let it dangle in the current. Also, don't hide the hook point in the chunk. Let the point protrude prominently for best penetration upon hook set. Before placing the chunk in the water make a final inspection to insure no bunker scales are stuck on the hook point.

My standard chunking rig again employs a fish finder rig. However, I use a relatively short leader (about 36 to 40-inches) so it is easier to cast the rig out into the slick. I prefer Berkley Big Game 40-pound monofilament for my main line when chunking because it stands up better to sticky structure and it cuts down the likelihood that the stripers will feel the rod and reel tension from the other end of the line.

Spice the Chunks:

There are ways to spice the baits up when fishing with frozen bunker. Bunker oil is readily available from area bait shops, and I use the oil to marinate the chunks on the way to the fishing grounds. There are also many manufacturers that produce other fish attractants. My favorite attractants come from a company called BioEdge. Many flavors are available, including bunker, and the scents come in both liquid and stick (balm) form. Either let the bunker chunks absorb some scent while soaking in the liquid, or use the stick to rub the smell on the chunks.

Another option is a little strange, but it works. Many years ago my brother Pete and I were fishing with Captain John Alberda out of Huntington Harbor. The action was fast and it was tough to keep up with the aggressively feeding stripers. However, bluefish eventually took over and quickly decimated our supply of fresh chunks. John had some left over bunker in the cooler, and although they were never frozen, these bunker had certainly seen better days. Well...even the bluefish seemed turned off by these stale chunks.

Out of the corner of my eye I saw John grab a can of WD-40,

and liberally spray down his bait. John tossed the chunk into the water and once it hit bottom it was immediately inhaled by a decent striper. In a flash, all our baits were sprayed with WD-40, and sent to the bottom. Bingo… the bite was re-ignited.

Chumming Ignites the Bite:

Seeding the area with pieces of bunker, while fishing chunk baits near the bottom, enhances the frequency of the bites. Cut up a couple of bunker into small pieces and throw them around the boat so they settle close by on the bottom.

The head and two chunks behind it are the best baits to place on the hook. The remaining two pieces are best used as chum chunks.

The scent from the chunks will draw in any bass that are in the area. It is best to chum at the beginning or end of a tidal period when the current is running slower. Chumming is less effective when the current is running fast because the pieces end up too far away from the boat. Also, there is a fine line between chumming too heavily and too lightly. I suggest avoiding chumming too heavily because this ends up feeding lazy bass lurking deep back in the slick, or attracting undesirable species such as skates, crabs, and dogfish.

Circle Hooks and Dead Sticking:

"Dead sticking" with circle hooks is the best bet for hooking up consistently with bunker chunks. I prefer dead sticking because moving a bunker chunk as a bass is about to eat it is the worst thing a fisherman can do. Remember, bass can be finicky eaters, and for some reason, this can be worse when bass are feeding on bunker chunks. If a bass senses anything wrong with a chunk it will immediately drop it. In addition, bass will sometimes pick up and drop the chunk several times before swallowing it. If the angler is holding the rod during this cat and mouse game, it is inevitable the angler will strike at the wrong time. I like to dead stick by putting the rod in a holder with the reel spool locked up. When the rod bends in half from a bucking striper, I take the rod out of the holder and fight the fish.

Capt. Dead Stick does it again.

Wire Line Instead of Sinkers:

Some anglers use wire line to get bunker chunks down near the bottom. This tactic is especially productive in areas with strong currents or over a very sticky bottom. If you want to try it, add a barrel swivel to the end of the wire line outfit and attach a 6 to 10-ft leader of 60-pound leader material. Finish the rig with a J-hook. Bait up, place the chunk in the water, put the reel clicker on, and slowly pull wire line off the reel. Be sure to pull the wire slowly enough so the current keeps the line tight, yet fast enough so the line and chunk slowly sinks. Stop letting out line when the bait is touching bottom. Take a few cranks to get the bait off the bottom, and when a solid tug is felt set the hook immediately.

Bunker baits have long been used to catch quality striped bass. This technique is simple and basic. However, if you use some of the tips I've just outlined I'm sure your success with big bass will certainly see a nice bump up.

Chunky striped bass like these two specimens are common when using bunker as bait.

Chapter 13

Striper Nectar - Clam Chum

Many years ago while fishing with Captain Al Ristori, he opined to me that clam juice is "nectar of the gods" to striped bass. Over the years I have come to appreciate his words because clam chumming is often a sure bet to catch lots of striped bass.

Al Ristori watches my buddy, Jack Fox, battle a bass to the boat anchored on Romer Shoal.

Clam chumming is especially popular with anglers that fish the Long Island south shore inlets. Here, it is especially productive after a storm has riled up the seas. A heavy surf cracks open a vast amount of clams, and striped bass will quickly move into the shallows to feed on the easy pickings.

There are important factors to keep in mind when fishing in the inlets. Inlets can be volatile places because vast amounts of water are funneled in and out, causing currents to move at an accelerated rate. Faster current is a main reason why striped bass feed in the inlets. But, when winds against current conditions develop dangerous sea conditions can quickly build. A little white water can be a good thing for striper fishing because water turbulence causes prey to struggle. However, always be cautious when fishing an inlet, when it looks too rough to fish, it probably is. Don't take chances because there will always be other days when conditions are safer to fish.

Anchor Correctly:

Better action is associated with anchoring up and chumming near sand bars and abrupt bottom changes. Never anchor in an inlet where you will be a hazard to navigation. Fortunately, much of the better bass action occurs on the channel edges where it is easy to find an anchoring spot out of the way. Anchoring properly requires adequate sized ground tackle (correct sizes of anchor, chain, and line) for the boat. If in doubt about the gear, check with a local boating supply store.

Be sure to anchor safely well in front of white water breaking on a bar.

Bait Clams and Chum Clams:

The clams used for chumming are Atlantic Surf Clams. Bait shops offer them for sale in a couple of varieties. I like to buy bushels of fresh, shucked, salted clams to use as hook bait. If fresh clams are not available, frozen clams will do. I prefer salted clams because salt toughens up the bait, and it is harder for bass to rip off them off the hook. I purchase my shucked clams by the bushel because it is the most economical way, and any leftovers may be frozen for the next trip.

Clam bellies are most often used as chum, but sometimes are also used as hook baits. When clams are harvested for either human consumption or as bait, the meaty parts are separated from the belly parts. Clam bellies are the non-muscle organs of the clams, and they are sold as clam belly chum.

Method 1:

Buy the clam bellies the day before the trip and allow them to defrost. Once anchored up safely on a channel edge or in front of a sand bar, it is time to get dirty. Grab a glob of clam bellies in your hand, hold them over the side of the boat, and squeeze the juices into the current. Once most of the juices have been dispersed, drop the remainder of the clam into the current. Grab another glob and repeat. The key to successful chumming is to establish a steady stream of clam chum into the tide without putting too much bait in the water. Once the slick is established, maintain it at a steady pace. A steady chum slick is doubly important after the bite starts.

Big bass like this aren't common on clam baits, but on occasion they will find a well presented clam bait to their liking..

Method Two:

A second chumming version is a little cleaner and hands free. With this method, don't allow the clam bellies to defrost. Instead, put the whole block of frozen clams into a square, weighted, chum pot. These pots or cages are available at tackle shops, and a 2-gallon block of frozen clam bellies fits perfectly inside the correct size cage. The cage can either be hung over the side of the boat at mid-depth or on the bottom. As the chum thaws, pieces of clams will peel off into the current and will attract the attention of feeding bass in the area.

Method 3:

Another option is to purchase frozen ground up clam chum. I suggest buying the chum in larger 3 to 5-gallon buckets. Take an old sturdy knife, cut out frozen chunks, and place the clams hunks into a fine mesh chum pots normally used for flounder or porgy fishing. Tether the pot to a line, lower it the bottom, and let the clams disperse into the current. Disadvantages of a small chum pot are the need to add chum frequently. Feel free to use any of the chumming methods in conjunction to get the stripers feeding in the chum slick.

Baiting Up:

I use both clam bellies and the meaty clam baits on my hooks. As mentioned, the fresh salted clams are tougher, and will stay on the hook more effectively. In spite of this, there will be times when the bass will show a preference for the softer bellies. Use both types of baits to see if there is any favorite on that tide. When I bait up with a meaty clam, I like to take the foot section, and hook it once at the very tip of the meat. I also add the longer stringy piece of meat to the hook point. The result is a bait that is about 8-inches long and when placed in the water streams enticingly in the current.

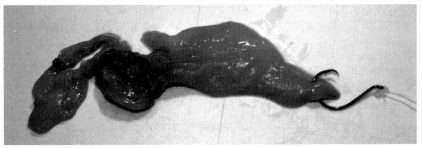

For the best presentation with a whole clam bait don't "ball" the bait up on the hook. First hook it at the very tip of the foot.

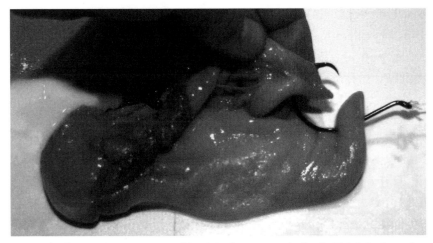

Next, take the stringy vent piece, and hook it also once on the hook. This helps keep the bait on the hook longer.

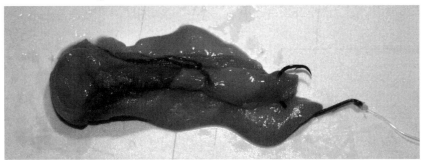

Baiting with a defrosted clam belly is like trying to put a lump of gook on the hook, and it's difficult to keep the bait on the hook. The best approach is to weave the belly on to the hook a few times and hope it stays on the hook long enough to catch a bass. I normally give each piece of bait 10-minutes of soak time before changing it for a another, "stinkier" one.

Rigging Up:

I usually present my clam baits on the fish finder rig. Keep in mind, sometimes it pays to deploy a rod with a three-way rig that has a 3-ft length of line as the sinker tether. Both rigs are outlined in chapter 8. I normally use a 3-ft piece of 40 to 60-pound leader for my hook leader. I prefer the "shorter" leader because the majority of the bass caught with clam baits are school stripers, up to 20-pounds. Keep in mind, one drawback of clam chumming is the possibility of a deeply hooked striper. To mostly avoid this problem, I highly suggest using circle hooks.

Spread the Baits:

Fan out baits in the slick. Inlet bass usually cruise just off the bottom in search of a meal. The best way to fool these bass is "dead sticking" a clam, weighted to the bottom, with a 6 to 8-ounce sinker. However, sometimes bass enter the slick at various depths. To catch these bass I like to suspend baits at different depths. This presentation is done by removing the fish finder rig and attaching a hook and leader to the barrel swivel at the end of the main line. Place various sized rubber core weights, or split shots, onto the main line, just above the barrel swivel. Put the clam bait in the water and let the current pull it away from the boat. As line comes off the reel, lightly thumb the spool to avoid an overrun. Upon a bass pick up, the main line will quickly peel off the reel. Continue to lightly thumb the spool, count to five, and engage the clutch on the reel to set the hook.

After a pick-up on a free floated clam let the bass run for a count of five.

Patience is good, but…

Schools of bass are constantly moving in and around inlets, so you never know when a school will be attracted to the chum slick. As a result, clam chumming can go from real slow to real fast in a flash. I prefer to clam chum on an outgoing current because this tide offers the best chance of attracting the attention of bass that are staging in the mouth of an inlet. Although exercising some patience is wise, don't waste an entire tide at an unproductive spot, and if the action is really slow a decision will have to be made. The options are to either drift around the inlet dragging the clam baits along the bottom, or to move somewhere else where bass might be feeding.

The inside of inlets are great places to fish clam baits for stripers.

Other Scenarios:

Commercial clam boats are common sights off our coast. These boats pull dredges along the bottom to scoop up surf clams. Inadvertently, clams will be cracked open and missed by the dredge. Striped bass will quickly flock into these areas and gobble down the clams. To cash in on this situation, simply make a few drifts down tide of a clam boat, but please use common sense and don't get in the way of the commercial guys.

Clam chumming works well around inlet bridges. Stripers love bridges and commonly lie in the lee of bridge abutments out of the current. These bridge bass can often be coaxed to bite with clam chum. When fishing the bridges on night tides, the hot zones are often the shadow lines created by the street lights on the bridge. Bass often lurk in the shadows, facing into the current, waiting for prey to wash by.

Bridges are striper magnets.

Within the bays there are marsh drains that attract and hold striped bass. These areas are especially productive in springtime when bay waters are cooler. Like inlets, these drains set up natural chum slicks on ebb tides when bait fish are pulled from deep inside the marshes. Anchor in deeper water off a drain, get the chum over the side, and cast clam baits to the area around the drain.

The Alavanja's with a nice school bass landed in Jones Inlet.

Remember, wherever a rip forms on the surface, there is a bottom change below that can attract bass. The back bays and channels are full of lightly fished rips, and under the right conditions, these spots can save the day.

Clam chumming is mostly a catch and release fishery. It's best to leave the light tackle home so the stripers can be landed quickly. Clam chumming has long been a method to put large numbers of striped bass in the boat.   Half the fun of a day's fishing is getting bites, and when clam chumming for stripers, you are certainly likely to get lots of bites.

Chapter 14

Casting and Jigging Lures

The most productive times to catch stripers on lures are during the spring and fall migrations when stripers are constantly on the move and aggressively feeding. Aggressively feeding stripers are always easier to fool with an artificial lure.

Jack Fox jigged up this beautiful striper in Montauk's North Rip.

Spinning rod and bait casting combos can be used successfully to present lures to feeding bass. To cover your bases, it pays to have both types of outfits onboard. Spinning gear is more appropriate for lighter lures that probe the upper half of the water, and bait casting gear is better suited for working heavier lures down deeper.

I don't think spinning rods are good choices for day to day big bass angling from a boat. I'm not saying big bass can't be landed on spinning tackle, but for the most part it is going to be a longer fight. Keep in mind, when using a spinning outfit it is vital not to crank the reel handle against the drag while the striper is making a run. Cranking at this time will cause line twists in the main line and weaken the line, causing "wind-knots" when casting. Hold the rod tip high during the striper's run, and let the bass take line from the reel drag during a run. Once the run stops, move the fish back to the boat with simultaneous pumps of the rod and cranks on the reel.

Don't turn the handle when a striper is taking line off a spinning reel.

Sunrise-Sunset:

Scientists have reported that striped bass and bluefish feed more actively under low light conditions such as sunrise and sunset. This is not to say that action will never occur on a sunny day at high noon. However, it is best to time casting trips on the water for bass either early or late in the day for the best chance at consistent action.

Every trip, when the sun gets in this position, I feel the bites are imminent.

Look for Birds:

It's often easy to find feeding bass by looking for wheeling and diving birds. Birds are nature's fish-finders and they will usually be first on the scene when bait is pushed to the surface by schools of fish. If there is a lot of surface activity, don't hesitate to throw surface swimmers or poppers because visual explosions on these types of lures always turn up the fun factor. The best lures to use are always those that match the size of the bait stripers are feeding on.

Birds equal bait. Baits equal bass.

Big Baits, Use Big Plugs:

The presence of big baits such as bunker, herring, or mullet makes large swimming plugs effective. I've had success with 6-inch Danny Metal Lip Swimmers, Super Strike Darters, Bomber A-Salts, and RedFin Swimmers. New plugs constantly come on the market that look real enough to fillet, so prowl the aisles of tackle shops to add to your arsenal. White or silver plugs match the colors of most baitfish, but blue plugs are great when bass feed on mullet in September. Orange and pink are great when squid are around in

This orange Danny did the trick when the bass were feeding on squid.

numbers. Yellow seems to turn the trick when baby weakfish or blowfish are the dominant prey.

Get in the habit of "working" the plug as opposed to "retrieving" the plug. This means, slow down and pay attention to the plug while it is swimming. Most surface swimming plugs are more productive when retrieved slowed enough to produce a V-wake behind the lure.

Stripers this size leave a huge hole in the water when they strike a popper.

Poppers:

Poppers are fun to use because the angler can see the fish striking the lure. Poppers are also great to probe a section of water for stripers. Even if a bass isn't caught, the popper might produce a surface strike letting you know there are fish in the area. It is best to retrieve the popper slowly so it sloshes and gurgles along the surface. Winging the lure out and zipping it back, skimming along the surface, rarely will catch anything but bluefish. Make the popper look like an injured prey having trouble swimming. In addition, do not set the hook on the explosive surface strike. Hesitate a second or so before rearing back on the rod, this insures the plug is in the fish's mouth, and will help improve the hook-up ratio. Super Strike Little Neck Poppers are a favorite of mine and I get most action on the 1-½ and 2-3/8-ounce sizes in white or yellow.

More Bass down Deep:

For every fish spotted on the surface under diving birds there will be countless more down deep. If fishing in relatively shallow water, say 10 to 20-ft, bucktails and weighted plastic swimbaits are very productive. I especially like swimbaits by Berkley, Storm, and Tsunami. Three to 4-inch swimbaits are good when bass are feeding on spearing or sand eels. If stripers are feeding on bunker or herring, go with 5 to 6-inch sizes. Plastic swimbaits definitely have a lot of built-in buoyancy, so it is often best to let the lure sink for a couple of seconds before beginning

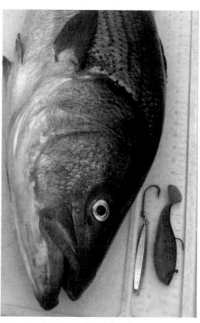

Diamond jigs and weighted swimbaits are excellent lures for most of the season.

a retrieve. Don't use a swimbait that has been maimed by a bluefish because it will not swim effectively.

I simply cast swimbaits and let the paddle tail produce the same type of vibration that pork rind does. Some anglers add scent attractants to the plastic swimbait. This can easily be done by using the balm type applicator from Bio Edge.

Diamond Jigs:

Diamond jigs are normally the lures I use when I'm marking stripers on the fish-finder in water 25-ft and deeper. Diamond jigs are especially productive when the main forage is sand eels, spearing, or anchovies. The correct size jig to use is one that will get the jig to the bottom with minimal line scope in the main line. In addition, the correct size will change according to the strength of the current. At Montauk, 4 to 8-once jigs will be needed to correctly fish an entire tidal stage.

Diamond jigs can also be worked quite effectively at any level of the water column. The jig can be dropped to the bottom to work the depths, or it can be retrieved immediately on splash down to work the surface. Although braided line works okay for jigging, I prefer monofilament as the main line because this line helps give the lure more flutter that results in a more productive presentation for striped bass.

Usually I prefer diamond jigs without tubes, but sometimes a tube makes the difference.

I usually prefer hammered finished jigs without tubes. The hammered jigs reflect more light compared to smooth-finished jigs. Diamond jigs with tubes have their times to shine, especially when big bait dominates, or when bass show a preference for a certain color. Green tubes seem to turn the trick when bass are on sand eels. White or red tubes work well when bass are feeding on anchovies, and squid. Sometimes silver jigs produce, sometimes it's the gold ones, so be sure to have both colors aboard.

There are other types of metal jigs that are called tins. These lures come in various shapes and usually have flat sides that will cause them to flutter more, drop slower in the water, and run shallower when retrieved. When bass are feeding on small porgies or butterfish, flat sided jigs can make a big difference.

Flatter sided tins can be the ticket to success when small porgies or butterfish are on the stripers menu.

Squidding:

A technique known as "squidding" is often the most

productive technique when diamond jigging. Reels with retrieves of 4 to 1 or higher are normally preferred by most serious jiggers. To "squid" properly, use a jig heavy enough to the reach bottom quickly, but not so heavy that it drops through the water like a stone. A diamond jig that flutters and wobbles as it falls, will always produce best. Fluttering reflects light, and feeding stripers often find this appearance very appealing. In fact, a striper will often pounce on a fluttering jig well before it reaches bottom. This type of bite is tough to feel. However, watch the line come off the reel as the jig falls. Upon a bass pick-up, the line will "jump" off the spool, and when this occurs, quickly engage the reel and strike hard.

Once the jig hits bottom, engage the reel and take up 10-quick turns on the reel handle, if any resistance is felt, strike hard to set the hook. After 10-turns drop down and hit the bottom again, and repeat the 10-cranks. Keep repeating this retrieve until either a hook up occurs or until the scope in the line is so great that the jig can no longer be felt touching the bottom. Once this happens reel the jig back to the boat and start over.

William "Doc" Muller fights a nice striper he hooked "squidding" a diamond jig.

Doc unhooks this nice June striper for a quick release.

Yo-Yo or Butter-flying:

Some anglers like to impart a yo-yo or butterfly action to the diamond jigs. The jig is dropped to the bottom, and when the jig touches down the reel is engaged and the lure is cranked a few feet off the bottom. Now sweep the rod in 3 ft-arcs, letting the jig flutter back down. When the jig stops, and tension is again felt on the main line, the sweeping action is repeated. This presentation is very successful at keeping the jig right off the bottom for an extended period of time, but with this presentation the jig hook will eventually fold over on the leader and tangle. When this happens it's time to reel up and untangle the jig.

Diane Mallahy used a Fin Nor reel to jig up this Block Island striper.

Stemming the Tide:

Stemming the tide with a diamond jig is a deadly presentation for big stripers, but it takes practice to get it right. The theory behind stemming the tide is to position the boat up current of a productive piece of bottom, and to point the bow of the boat into the current. Keep the boat in gear with just enough forward speed to hold the vessel pretty much stationary in the current. Drop the diamond jig to the bottom, touch bottom, and engage the reel. Take 5 s-l-o-w turns on the reel handle. This will cause the diamond jig to leisurely rise off the bottom, and to tremble and wobble in the water pressure created by the current. If a bite is not felt after the 5-turns are complete, drop down, touch the bottom, and repeat the 5 s-l-o-w turns. Keep repeating this process until either a hook up occurs, or the jig is no longer felt touching bottom. Reel up, and re-position the boat and repeat the process. Experiment with jig sizes to get the right action. Sometimes, it pays to use heavier leader material such as 80 or 100-pound test. The thicker leader size will help to "float" the lure, and make the jig more tempting to a striper.

Bucktails:

Casting bucktails from a boat produces very good action

A yellow Spro bucktail , and red pork rind was the undoing of this fine school bass.

with assorted sizes of striped bass. This can be done on the drift, but in my opinion the best way is to anchor up-tide of a rip or boulder field, and to cast the bucktail back over fertile structure.

As mentioned in chapter 10, I prefer white bucktails with Smiling Bill heads, but most styles of bucktails will be productive when casting. Sometimes, bucktails with a free swinging hook have a slight edge when casting bucktails over bucktails with fixed hooks. Once again, always use a pork rind trailer as an attractant to the hook.

Bucktail weight and pork rind size is important when casting. The bucktail should be retrieved near the bottom, but not dragging along it. The bucktail size will depend on current and water

Changing the size of the pork rind slice will alter it's cast ability, and sink rate.

depth. If the bucktail bumps bottom, go lighter. If the bucktail runs too high in the water, go heavier. I normally use Uncle Josh's 70-S pork rind, but sometimes a thinner rind like the 240-S will allow more casting distance, and depth to the jig. When necessary, let the bucktail sink for a few seconds before starting the retrieve. A slow and steady retrieve seems to produce best, but sometimes a few hops, or hesitations, will trigger bites too.

As you face the water, cast the bucktail to approximately a 9-O'clock position relative to the current. I let the bucktail drift for a few seconds, so it can sink into the current, and when the lure is at the 10-O'clock position I begin my retrieve. Most bites will come between 11-O'clock and 2-O'clock on the swing. When the angle of the line reaches 3-O'clock, I speed up the retrieve to get the lure back to the boat for another cast. It will be necessary to constantly change the weights of the bucktails depending on the strength of current.

As mentioned, I normally cast or jig lures only when bass are tightly schooled during their annual migrations. However, the attention to detail needed for consistent success when casting or jigging, will go a long way towards making you a better all around angler. In addition, it's simply a lot of fun feeling that solid "thump" when a bass pounces on a lure. It's truly one of the great joys in striper fishing.

Stripers are suckers for many types of lures, and that's a main reason why they are such a popular game fish.

Chapter 15

Nighttime Tips

Although I love fishing for striped bass anytime, anyplace, my juices really flow when I'm out on night tides. Night striper fishing is both tranquil and thrilling, and I have cherished these trips ever since my first night trip with Captain Bob Rocchetta many years ago.

On night trips, stripers like this one caught on the Miss Mac, *are a common catch. Photo: Capt. Pete Mikoleski.*

I can hear the naysayers now, "But Captain Tom we fished with *Capt. Bill* on an August day trip and we killed the bass." Yes, I agree, big bass are caught on day trips also. In fact, during July of 2012, I experienced a span of days with huge bass aggressively feeding midday on very weak tides. I can't explain why it happened, but it did. That being said, striped bass are nocturnal by nature. Darkness is an advantage for them because their eyes have evolved to gather light efficiently, even in darkness. Also, at night big stripers are less skittish and are more likely to school up to aggressively feed. These are the reasons why I feel any night, could be the night, I land the striper of my dreams.

Not quite the striper of my dreams, but the smile says it all.

Safety First:

Striped bass fishing at night from a boat has some inherit dangers. However, with today's navigation electronics, fishing at night should not be something to fear. In spite of this, there are a few cautions to consider. Common sense dictates that it is best to learn the area during daylight before venturing out at night. Local knowledge of an area is always more accurate than any nautical chart. Also, make sure that the boat is in good operating condition. According to Murphy's Law, anything that can go wrong will go wrong at nighttime. Having proper safety gear is vital and includes all navigation lights and other safety equipment such as flares, life vests, and signal devices. It's also a good idea to carry several handheld flashlights with back-up batteries in case there is an electrical problem. Almost everyone has cell phones, and they are great for emergencies, but don't rely on them solely. Have a quality VHF radio aboard too. An EPIRB and inflatable life raft is also a great safety measure.

Capt. Erik Weingartner hoists a heft 44-pound striper landed aboard the Grand Slam *on a September full moon night.*

Electronics:

A good chart plotter and fish-finder are indispensable in order to make precise drifts. Nowadays, good units can be bought in the $500 to $1000 range. Radar is not necessary, but once you become familiar with it, you'll never leave the dock without one.

Please read the manuals that come with the units. I remember one early evening a few years ago when I was picking my way back to the dock in thick fog. Once I neared the vicinity of the Inner Shagwong Buoy off Montauk, the fog lifted. It was still light out, and with the improved visibility, I throttled up to 15-knots and proceeded to run for the inlet in a due west direction. Suddenly my mate came into the pilothouse and said, "Do you see that big sportfisher?" I turned to see a 48' sportfisherman fast approaching the port side. I was dumb struck because there was now plenty of visibility. I immediately turned hard to starboard and did a circle around the Shagwong buoy because I had no idea what this guy was up to. I continued on to the harbor and turned to see the sport fisherman slow down, and tuck in very close to my wake.

The sportfisherman was decked out with all the whiz-bang electronics money could buy. Still, I had no idea what the hell this captain was doing. In fact, neither did he. Once we got into the harbor I slowed to let him overtake us. I yelled up to his bridge, "What the hell was that all about?" He then thanked me for leading him into the harbor. I proceeded to explain that he had just scared the hell out of me and my passengers. Apparently, we had a captain with a multi-million dollar vessel, and all the electronics, but he could not find Montauk harbor from a distance of 2-miles away. That's pathetic. This goes to show, just because you can afford it, doesn't mean you can drive it.

Don't Go Dark:

No matter how confident you are in the dark, don't ever become a nighttime ninja and shut the lights off to avoid being seen.

This is both illegal and stupid. Collisions happen at night, heck they even happen during the day, but at night it's really the time to worry about the other guy. So always illuminate the vessel at night. In fact, when I run night charters my deck lighting is on for the entire trip and it provides all onboard with the luxury of seeing what they are doing.

Don't be a Nighttime Ninja, at least keep your navigation lights on.

Night Lighting:

Lighting will make the trip on the water much easier. I built my boat with through hull underwater lights. I don't normally leave these lights on while drifting, but once a fish is hooked I turn on the lights to make netting or gaffing easier. Don't worry about cockpit lights negatively affecting the fishing. I remember one night a few seasons ago when on a new moon it was dark as can be. My friends and I were drifting live eels in about 15-ft of water

Stripers are not shy to lights on boats, keep the cockpit lights on so all can see what the heck they are doing.

just off the Montauk Lighthouse. The fishing was good all evening, and on one drift we hooked three bass almost simultaneously. As I customarily do, I put the underwater lights on to assist landing the fish. I was leaning over the side to slip the net under a 35-pounder when I clearly spotted five other bass, swimming into the glow of the underwater lights. The bass were following the hooked fish I was netting, and their main focus was on the eel that was dangling out of the hooked fish's mouth. These five bass swam in the lights for a few seconds, and then slowly glided away into the darkness. Since that night I have no worries about my cockpit lights affecting the fishing.

Slow Down:

During night tides it is smart to navigate slowly. I can't tell you how many times I see boats zipping around at high speed, this is stupefying because I occasionally also see logs and other debris floating on the surface of the water. I often wonder if these full

Slow down and we can all catch nice stripers like this on night tides.

throttle heroes have ever seen the same hazards. For all the speed demons, please realize all the anglers out at night prefer things to be nice and quiet. So leave the weekend warrior attitude back at the dock. This also means watch the wake, because a large wake runs the risk of shutting the bite down for everyone.

Be Quiet:

Avoid noises such as dropping the anchor or chain, slamming shut a heavy fish box, or stamping your feet. These are not normal sounds to the bass and can shut the action down like an on-off switch. Also, be aware that voices carry a long way underwater.

I also suggest keeping the onboard stereo volume down low or off. One night I was fishing Jones Inlet on Long Island's South Shore. My crew and I had just landed a few nice bass on the edge of a channel that flowed close to the beach. Soon, another boat came from out of the dark and got right into my drift. No big deal, I thought, as the angler did it slowly and well in back of the drift, but, when he shut his engine off I could here "Free Bird" whaling from the speakers. I love this song as much as any other rocker, but come on...really? We went up for another drift and just like that, the fish-finder was bare and the bites ended. Could the bass have just left? Possibly, but I think it was more than likely that the wailing guitars sent the bass packing for a quieter feeding area.

Doc Muller with a chunky striper caught on a nice calm night. Don't tempt Mother Nature.

Weather Watch:

Look-out for strong storms passing through the area. Storms will kick up waves quickly. Cruising in heavy seas is never fun, but doing it at night with lightning bolts crackling above is downright scary. A little known fact about lightning is that if you are close enough to hear thunder, you are close enough to be struck by lightning...yikes!!

I recently purchased a Lowrance HDS chart plotter that has an option for real time weather radar through a Sirius Satellite weather module. I love this feature because I can clearly see thunderstorms approaching in real-time. In fact, I can even set an alarm for lightening strikes. I keep the unit's alarm set at 25-miles, and if it goes off I will closely monitor the weather screen to see if a run to the dock is warranted. Don't be stupid with thunderstorms, and besides, many times lightening will shut down the night bass bite in a "flash."

Bass like this feed best on strong currents. Strong currents running into a strong wind can create some nightmarish conditions. This is especially so in the darkness of the night.

Be Aware of the Conditions:

Fishing for stripers is often best in areas of strong current. Be on the lookout for wind-against-the-tide conditions that causes seas to build very quickly to dangerous levels. At Montauk, I usually fish the flood tide during the summer months when southwest winds are common. A southwest wind and a flood tide produce flat calm seas at the Point. Winds from the north or northwest above 15-knots on the flood tide, produces tight 4 to 6-ft seas from the lighthouse to the harbor. During daylight, these conditions are no big deal, but at night, it's no fun at all. It's prudent to know the effects of wind and tide on sea conditions in your area, and if in doubt, stay home. There will be plenty of other nights when conditions are more favorable.

Larry Moore bagged this beautiful bass on a foggy night in the North Rips off Montauk.

Fog:

I'm very leery of fog. Fog can be a problem at anytime of the day, but sometimes Radiation Fog develops at night. This occurs when moist air blows over a cooling surface (land or water) causing fog. Fog is common in most coastal areas so it is something you should be prepared to deal with. Again, I don't like fog, but if I stayed at the dock every time fog was in the forecast I'd be stuck at the dock for a good part of the season. I trust myself in the fog, but I don't trust the other guys. Neither should you. Keep your engine on so you can maneuver instantly, and always watch the radar screen. Please...be very careful in the fog.

Nighttime Tendencies:

Here are some generalities about night fishing for stripers that I have noticed. During a full moon period (3-days before and after a full moon) a pretty good bite often occurs a half hour before and after sunset, but sometimes the bite will shut down for a while until the moon rises in the sky.

"Fire" in the water did not stop this double header drift.

On the very dark night of the new moon a condition called "fire in the water" can develop. This happens when warm and calm conditions stimulate a bloom of dinoflagellates: a type of plankton.

This 45-pounder was caught as the sun set. However, once it got dark, the "fire" was visible, and the bite got pretty tough no matter what I tried to do.

When the phosphorescent planktons are churned up, a green glow can clearly be seen in the prop wash. The line, rig, and bait will also be taking on this subtle green glow. Often, the glow can interfere with the bite. Normally this condition is only a problem on very dark nights because moon light of any intensity will often be enough to "cancel out" the glow. To be honest, I have had some incredible nights with fire in the water, but I know many anglers believe it causes the stripers to shut down. If "fire" is a concern, "go light to get the bite", in order to reduce the agitation of the water around the rig. Lighten up on everything: line test, swivels, sinkers, hooks and lure or bait size. Moving the rig slower through the water will also help.

Be Prepared:

Tying rigs in darkness takes more time than normal. I suggest rigging up several extra rods, so if a rig is lost all you have to do to get back into the action is to take another rod out of the rack. I also keep my tackle organized in plastic compartment trays. I put swivels and hooks in the same position every time, so I can quickly grab what I need to re-rig.

A crew trip in June produced one nice fish each for Steve, Angel, and Kenny. Hey...where's mine?

Dress for Comfort:

It gets cool on the water at night, so always bring along a few extra layers of clothing. Rain gear bottoms and rubber boots will go a long way towards raising the comfort level. I don't recommend flip flops or bare feet whenever bass fishing and this goes double at night. In fact, I cringe severely whenever I see the "Florida Pros" on outdoor television shows walking around their boat's deck in bare feet. I know Florida is hot, but come on. One broken toe caused by a slip, and you're done for the trip. Over the years, I have accidently dropped a few big bass to the deck and the dorsal spines on these big girls can do serious damage to a foot. Luckily, I've only had a few close calls, but I have had bass spines puncture holes into my boats. Later on when changing to street shoes I have found a few bloody socks. I hate to think of the pain I would have been in had those spines deeply impaled my foot.

In my opinion, night tides are the right times to hunt big bass. However, if you are skittish about doing it alone don't hesitate to hire a professional to show you the ropes. If you have the gumption to do it alone, good look, and be safe. It probably won't be long before the aura and mystique of nighttime striper fishing captivates you as much as it has me.

Chapter 16

Increasing Survival Rates of Released Stripers

In a perfect world of striper management, any fish harvested from the fishery one season would be replaced in the next spawn. This is easier said than done because spawning success is mostly determined by environmental factors.

Getting them back into the water quickly is key to a successful release.

Stripers are tough, hardy fish. If they do not incur internal injuries during the fight with an angler, chances are they will survive the release. Major injuries are most likely to occur when bait fishing because a bass often swallows the bait whole. This can be problematic for anglers who use J-hooks because when an angler waits too long to set a J-hook it often becomes lodged in the striper's gullet. This problem can be greatly avoided by using circle hooks when bait fishing.

A striper that is deeply hooked still has a good chance at

surviving as long as the hook is not dug out, causing further injuries. The best thing to do with a deeply hooked striper is to cut the leader close to the hook and get the striper back into the water quickly. If the bass was not bleeding heavily, it will probably survive because the hook will quickly rust away. I have caught several striped bass over the years with hooks still in their mouth or gullet region and the fish always seemed healthy. In fact, the new world record striper caught by Greg Myerson in August of 2011 had two old hooks stuck in its mouth and throat area.

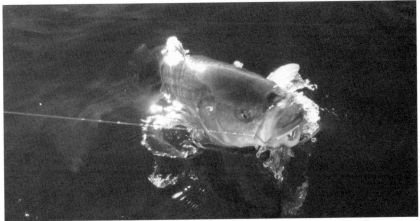

A circle hook is clearly seen penetrating the corner of the jaw of this 25-pounder.

Choosing the proper style and size circle hook will have an impact on the catch ratio. It is best to use circle hooks that have a very slight, or no offset hook point. This style of hook causes less damage even when a striper does swallow the hook. I feel many anglers use circle hooks that are too small for the huge mouth of the striped bass. As mentioned in chapter 8, I prefer 8/0 Circle hooks and I use this size whether I'm clam chumming, eel drifting, or bunker chunking and have caught stripers from 8 to 55-pounds with them.

The only time circle hooks don't work well is when a striper takes the bait and swims towards the boat, but I'll argue it would be tough to hook a striper in this case with any style hook.

Just how effective are circle hooks at avoiding deeply hooked stripers? A few years back I did my own experiment while anchored and clam chumming. I used 2-rods rigged with circle hooks on a fish finder rig. All hook ups came with my rod in a holder, with the

A striper that his all it's fins erect is a prime candidate for an easy release.

reel locked up, and the drag set properly. After a few trips I tallied over 100-stripers, and only five were deeply hooked. That's a pretty good average. However, I often wondered about the fish I released. One day while web surfing I found the following information.

In 1999 a study was conducted by the Maryland Department of Natural Resources. Multiple 2-day fishing trips were conducted from June to October within the confines of Chesapeake Bay. On the first day J-hooks were used, and on the second day non-offset circle hooks were deployed. Once a fish was caught Fisheries Service Biologists recorded the location of the hook wound by clipping the tail in a defined area. If the fish was deeply hooked, the hook was left in place and the leader cut.

The fish were placed in holding pens that had similar water

temperature, and salinity levels to where the bass were caught. The stripers were held in the pens for 72-hours and checked daily. All dead fish were removed, and those marked as deeply hooked had post mortem examinations conducted on them.

During the study, 476 striped bass were caught on traditional J-hooks, and 640 fish on the circle hooks. The size of the fish caught with both hooks ranged from 16.4-inches to 36.6-inches. The deep hooking rate for J-hook stripers was 17.2%, and for circle hooks 3.4%. Overall, 9.1% of the striped bass caught on J-hooks died. Only 0.8% of the striped bass caught on circle hooks expired. When post mortems were conducted on the deeply hooked stripers, caught on

A 30-pound striper is released by Joe Scalone on the Miss Mac.

J-hooks, it showed internal injuries caused by the hook points. The small percentage of deeply hooked stripers caught on circle hooks showed tears to the esophagus caused by the **outside** bend of the hook.

This study showed that circle hooks not only catch more fish, but they also result in less fatal injuries to striped bass. This should be enough information to encourage the switch to circle hooks when bait fishing for striped bass.

There have been other catch and release studies that indicate water temperature can play a role in the survivability of released striped bass. Water temperatures above 70-degrees have a negative effect on their survivability. For those of us who fish in the Northeast, temperatures this high only occur during August. So, common sense dictates a need to handle the fish more carefully and invest more time reviving them at this time of the season.

Tom Plantz seems happy with this nice striper caught and released in Montauk's North Rip.

Fishing with artificials rarely results in deeply hooked stripers, but treble hooks on plugs can cause damage. Crushing the barbs on the treble hooks will reduce injuries and quicken release time. The problem with crushing barbs is that a few bass are going to be lost during the fight.

Striped bass can also be injured by the stress caused from the exertion of the fight with an angler. The best way to reduce stress on a hooked striper is to end the fight quickly as possible. This is why I stress the importance of using proper sized fishing gear and appropriately set drag. The longer the fight, the less chance a striper has at surviving a release. Light gear just isn't sporting for the fish.

Once a bass is landed there are several things that an angler can do to help a released striper survive. If possible, unhook the striper without lifting it from the water. For many of us, like me, this is not an option because of high transoms.

What about the use of a net? Does netting hurt the bass? In my opinion it is better to lift a big bass into the boat with a net so its

Captain Erik prepares to release a nice 27-pound striper.

internal organs are supported by the net. Doesn't netting remove a striper's slime coat? I have never witnesses a build-up of slime in my net. Have you?

Once the striper is in the boat, turn on the saltwater wash down pump and pump some water on the deck. This creates a film of water between the striper and the deck. If the striper starts thrashing about, grab a clean rag, soak it in saltwater, and place it over the striper's eyes. This immediately calms the striper. Remove the hook quickly, so have gloves or unhooking devices close at hand. Avoid grasping the striper inside the gills, grabbing the hard outer gill plate is ok, but don't touch the red gills inside the plate.

Taking photos is fine, but have the camera ready. Taking pictures on the water, when the fish is vibrant, results in wonderful photos. Once you see how good these photos are, shots taken back at the dock, or worse, in the home driveway, won't cut it any longer.

Most small bass will not have to be revived because they are quickly cranked into the boat. Bigger stripers that fight long and hard will often need reviving. If the striper's dorsal fin is erect the bass will need minimal reviving. If the dorsal fin is limp, or the striper is in shock because of the build-up of lactic acid, the striper is going to need work.

Once the striper is back in the water hold it by the lower lip and rock the striper back and forth. This will push water through the gills. Usually, in a few seconds the striper will begin to clamp down on your thumb. This is a good sign, keep rocking. When the striper is ready to go it will pull away from your grasp, slap the water with its broad tail, and probably leave you with a face full of water as a goodbye salute.

If a striper can't be revived in 10 to 15-minutes, chances are the fish is not going to make it. Relish in the thought that you did your best. If you have a slot available for a keeper it's time to get the bass on ice. Whenever keeping any type of fish, the fillet will be

Hold the bass by the lip and rock the fish back and forth in the water. The striper will let you know when it's ready to go.

much firmer and less bloody if the fish is bled out. This is done by placing a knife blade into the rear of the gill plate and slicing down towards the underside of the fish.

If killing a big striped bass disgusts you, it might be best to pick another sport because there are times when fish are going to die. I do feel a twinge of regret when I dispatch a true cow, but I don't have a problem harvesting fish. However, I never take more than I need, and I never throw big ones on the dock just to impress the dock gawkers. I preach this same belief to my charter anglers. Sometimes it works, sometimes it doesn't, but I try. As for me, it is a good bet that if I harvest a fish today it will be cooked tonight or tomorrow because nothing beats fresh fish. Once used to fresh fish it's tough to eat the inferior product often available at fish markets.

Personally, I don't think it is a good idea to weigh a striper that is going to be released because hanging the bass unsupported on a scale by the gill plate or lip, can't be doing any good to the striper's organs. However, if you simply *must* weigh the fish, do as my friend Dr. Jim House of the North Fork Captains Association recommends, leave the striper in the net, and weigh the net and fish together. This way, the net basket will help support the striper's organs. Once done, simply minus the weight of the net from the total poundage.

There is another option to weighing. Simply carry a vinyl tape measure and by using the following mathematical formula a close estimate of the striper's weight can be gotten:
Girth X Girth X Length / 800

Calculating a 50-pound striper is done as so:
29-(inch girth) X 29-(inch girth) = 841. 841 X 51-(inch length) = 42,891 / 800 =53.6-pounds

You also don't need a dead fish to get a mount these days. Simply take the length and girth measurements punch them into the above formula, and call a local taxidermist and request a fiberglass replica mount of the trophy sized fish.

A big striped bass is released through the "striper door" on the Grand Slam.

"Game fish are too valuable to only be caught once." -
Lee Wulff

Chapter 17

Closing Thoughts

Tides and Currents:

Specific stages of a tide or current can turn the fishing action on, or off like a switch. Accordingly, understanding how tides and currents influence the feeding tendencies of stripers are keys to becoming a better striper angler.

Tidal movement is the vertical rise and fall of sea level caused by the gravitational relationship between the earth, sun, and moon. The northeast coast goes from low tide to high tide in about 6-hours. Two high or low tides occur about 12-hours and 25-minutes apart. In order for the water height to change, a force (gravity) must develop to push the water, and the result of the change in water level is current.

Current is the horizontal movement of water that flushes bays and harbors. Fortunately for anglers, currents move baitfish. Predator fish seek areas where current concentrates baitfish. A strongly flowing current allows predator fish, like stripers, too easily pick off baitfish.

Moon Tides:

I mentioned "moon" tides previously in chapter 9. However, here is a more in depth explanation of why these tides are so productive for striped bass. A "moon" tide is more accurately called a "spring" tide. This is when the gravitational force of a new or full moon pulls extra hard on ocean waters resulting in higher and lower tides. Between spring tides the vertical difference between high and low tides is less and is called "neap" tides. Striper fishing is usually good on moon/spring tides because the amount of time it takes to go

Steve Phillip's with almost a fifty.

from high to low tide is still approximately 6-hours. For tides to get higher or lower in the same time frame, current flow must increase. As a result, 7-days of good striped bass fishing normally occur on "moon" periods.

I don't have a preference for either the new or full moon periods. However, I have noticed a tendency for good action to stretch 5-nights after the moon. To take advantage of this pattern, be on the water late at night when the stronger parts of the currents occur.

Structure:

Fish are attracted to various structure and this goes double with striped bass. Structures can be any of the following: bridges, sand bars, inlets, creek mouths, harbor entrances, jetties, natural reefs, artificial reefs, wrecks, points of land, boulder fields, channel edges, mussel beds, and dock lines. This is quite an assortment, but they will all hold stripers at some point during the season. Fish structures consistently, and you will catch lots of striped bass.

A sandy hill off Montauk's north side produced this beautiful striped bass.

Charts:

Don't discount the value of nautical charts to find new structures in the areas you fish. I spend a good part of each off-season looking over nautical charts. I look for steep depth changes, or bottom characteristics marked on charts as mussel beds and sand waves. I figure approximate latitude and longitude numbers and give these spots a try when stripers are in the area. Often this homework pays off.

A tiny rock pile I found on a chart produced this double header of striper's that weighed between 35 and 41-pounds.

Little Things Count:

Large stripers are survivors that have run the gauntlet along the coast for anywhere from 15 to 30-years. In that span, big stripers have had lots of lures and baits thrown their way. So, when hunting big bass, little things matter. In order to consistently hook big bass an angler has to be on his game at all times. This means being ready for a striper bite when it happens. Over the years, how many bites have you missed? I know I've definitely missed my fair share. In reality, each missed bite could have been from "the striper" we've all been searching for our whole fishing lives.

Mike DiGregorio is always ready for "the bite," the result is, he often is high-hook on the trip.

Why Sport Fisherman Love Them:

Commercial fishermen never seem to "get it" when it comes to the striped bass. They simply see stripers as revenue for their wallets. For sport fisherman in the Northeast or Mid-Atlantic Region, the view is very different. The striped bass is "the fish" to catch when looking to land a truly large fish. In relation, a cow striper is "our" tarpon, giant bluefin, goliath grouper, or swordfish. Truthfully, if I could go out and catch any of these other fish from my home inshore waters, I would. But, I can't. So for me, and millions of other anglers, the striped bass has become all those other game fish wrapped into one package.

To further illustrate how special stripers are to sport fishermen, let me relate the following story. One day on my dock, the mate from a nearby boat that specializes in both chartering and pin hooking for porgies came over to me and started a conversation. To paraphrase, here's what was said to me, "What is it about the striped bass that makes people crazy? Today we caught our limit of porgy pretty easily, and then the charter group asked to fish for stripers. We ran to the rips and almost immediately hooked up with a few 25 to 30-pound stripers. Nice fish, nothing incredible, but I couldn't believe the reaction of these people on the charter. They were all whooping, hollering, and smiling ear to ear. I've never seen such a reaction to a damn fish!" I simply replied, "Well, now you know why we fish for them, and why we love them."

This prime breeder was released by Capt. Wayne October 2012. Hopefully she will add millions of eggs to the spawn for many years to come.

The fight after a hook-up with a large striper is the payoff for all the long hours invested into the pursuit. As the years have gone by, I've learned to cherish each fight because in the scheme of things, one never knows when their last striper is in fact...***their last striper.*** By now, my obsession with striped bass should be abundantly clear. However, nowhere on these pages has it been written that I enjoy killing these beautiful fish. In fact, the only rush greater than landing a big one, is releasing a big one.

I hope with my guidance all of you become better striped bass anglers. In spite of this, don't ever become a striped bass hog. It isn't necessary to keep your limit every time you reach it. It's also a good practice to release many of the big striped bass you catch, so they can live, breed, and fight another day.

Full disclosure, as a charter boat captain I do help harvest a lot of big stripers, but I also do my best to educate anglers about how important striped bass are to all who fish for them. In fact, I have a sign posted on my boat that reads:

Dear Anglers:

You have paid a lot of money for this charter. I have no problem with the keeping of any legal sized striper that is within the bag limit. Please keep in mind, almost every striped bass over 20-pounds is a female capable of spawning millions of eggs next spring. By practicing catch and release with large stripers you are helping to insure good fishing will be available for future generations of anglers.

During much of the season, I witness firsthand the tremendous pressure put on the striped bass. Striper fishing was once a fishery made up of a relatively small number of dedicated anglers. Now, an unprecedented number of anglers are involved in the fishery. In my opinion, because of this pressure, it might be time to reduce the annual harvest. I say this with crossed fingers, hoping it won't hurt my growing charter business. Nevertheless, in my heart

I know a healthy striped bass fishery is more important to me than my striper charter business.

The Grand Slam *cruising on a beautiful August day.*

My boat, *Grand Slam* is located at the fine facility *Gone Fishing Marina*, 467 East Lake Drive, Montauk, NY 11954. *Gone Fishing* has a shop for all your boating and fishing needs, including transient slips, and a pay per use boat ramp. The entire staff is well tuned into the fishing and weather forecasts, so when in Montauk don't hesitate to call or stop by to stock up on information or supplies.

Ninety percent of my business is word of mouth and repeat customers. Anglers who fish with me know I do my best to get them into fish, and I don't B.S. them. If the weather is bad or the fishing stinks, I'll inform them. Sometimes we reschedule and sometimes we give it a go, I leave it up to the charter to decide, and this honesty is appreciated. I also never force my customers to "drag" wire to just throw stripers on the dock.

I thoroughly enjoyed writing this book, and no where in it did I pound my chest and proclaim, "I'm the best striper fisherman in Montauk." This is because, I'm not. However, I work my butt off for my customers to catch stripers. Usually I'm successful, but sometimes I'm not. I guess that's why it's called fishing and not catching. So, on that note...*good catching* to all.

Stay safe, and thank you for reading about my great angling passion. I hope you did in fact...*enjoy the ride* into my striper obsession.

EPILOGUE

    If there are any questions pertaining to techniques outlined in this book, or to book a charter aboard the *Grand Slam*, I can be reached at 516-457-5298. Obviously, I'm a striped bass specialist, but I also fish for fluke, sea bass, porgies, blackfish, and sharks. I'm also available for fishing seminars at clubs, shows, and other gatherings. To join my customer e-mail list, where special charters, open trips, and fishery updates are posted please e-mail me at:

GrandSlamCharter@aol.com

My website can be viewed at
www.MontaukStriperFishing.com.

Best Regards,
Capt. Tom Mikoleski